World Religions Reference Library Cumulative Index

World Religions Reference Library Cumulative Index

CUMULATES THE INDEXES FOR

WORLD RELIGIONS: ALMANAC,

WORLD RELIGIONS: BIOGRAPHIES, AND

WORLD RELIGIONS: PRIMARY SOURCES

Julie L. Carnagie, Index Coordinator

U·X·L
An imprint of Thomson Gale,
a part of The Thomson Corporation

THOMSON
™
GALE

Detroit • New York • San Francisco • New Haven, Conn. • Waterville, Maine • London

THOMSON
GALE

World Religions Reference Library Cumulative Index

Project Editor
Nancy Matuszak

Editorial
Julie L. Carnagie

Rights and Acquisitions
Edna Hedblad, Emma Hull, Sue Rudolph

Imaging and Multimedia
Lezlie Light, Dan Newell, Christine O'Bryan, Robyn Young

Product Design
Jennifer Wahi

Composition
Evi Seoud

Manufacturing
Rita Wimberley

LIBRARY OF CONGRESS CATALOGING-IN-PUBLICATION DATA

Jones, J. Sydney.
World religions reference library / edited by Neil Schlager and Jayne Weisblatt; written by J. Sydney Jones and Michael O'Neal; Nancy Matuszak, content project editor.
p. cm. -- (World religions reference library)
Includes bibliographical references and index.
ISBN-13: 978-1-4144-0227-7 (Almanac : set : alk. paper) --
ISBN-10: 1-4144-0227-9 (Almanac : set : alk. paper) --
ISBN-13: 978-1-4144-0228-4 (Almanac : vol. 1 : alk. paper) --
ISBN-10: 1-4144-0228-7 (Almanac : vol. 1 : alk. paper) --
[etc.]
1. Religions. I. O'Neal, Michael, 1949- II. Schlager, Neil, 1966- III. Weisblatt, Jayne.
IV. Title.V. Series.
BL74.J66 2006
200--dc22

2006012295

ISBN-13:

978-1-4144-0229-1 (Almanac vol. 2)	978-1-4144-0232-1 (Biographies vol. 2)
978-1-4144-0230-7 (Biographies set)	978-1-4144-0232-8 (Primary Sources)
978-1-4144-0231-4 (Biographies vol. 1)	978-1-4144-0234-5 (Cumulative Index)

ISBN-10:

1-4144-0229-5 (Almanac vol. 2)	1-4144-0232-5 (Biographies vol. 2)
1-4144-0230-9 (Biographies set)	1-4144-0233-3 (Primary Sources)
1-4144-0231-7 (Biographies vol. 1)	1-4144-0234-1 (Cumulative Index)

This title is also available as an e-book.
ISBN-13: 978-1-4144-0232-1, ISBN-10: 1-4144-0612-6
Contact your Thomson Gale sales representative for ordering information.
Printed in the United States of America

10 9 8 7 6 5 4 3 2

Cumulative Index

A

Abbasids
  A *2:* 298, 299
Abdal-Rahman ibn Muhammad
  ibn Khaldūn. *See* ibn Khaldun
Abd-er-Rahman
  A *2:* 298
Abdu'l-Baha
  A *1:* 73–74, 76, 79 (ill.)
  PS 182
Abdul-Jabbar, Kareem
  A *2:* 300
Abdullah, Muhammad Ibn.
  See Muhammad
Abdullah (son of Muhammad)
  B *1:* 199
Abhaya mudra
  A *1:* 109
Abimelech
  B *1:* 6
Aborigines, creation stories of
  PS 3
Aborigines (Australia)
  A *2:* 271
Abraham
  A *2:* 346
  B *1:* 1(ill.), **1–8**
  PS 24
  descendants of
  B *1:* 6

early life
  B *1:* 2
expulsion from Egypt
  B *1:* 3–4
God's promises to
  B *1:* 5
influence of
  B *1:* 7–8
role in major religions
  B *1:* 1–2
similarities with Jesus Christ
  B *1:* 1
Abram. *See* Abraham
Abstinence
  A *1:* 141, 142
Abu Bakr (caliphh)
  A *2:* 298, 301
  B *1:* 18, 20
  PS 29
Abu Sufyan
  B *2:* 291
Abu Talib
  B *1:* 18, 200, 201
Abydos (Egypt)
  A *1:* 58–59
Academy of Plato
  B *2:* 316
Achaemenid dynasty
  A *2:* 447
Acharya
  B *2:* 235

Achyutapreksha
  B *2:* 235
Active learning
  B *2:* 215
Acts of Paul and Thecla
  B *2:* 302
Acts of the Apostles
  A *1:* 137
  B *2:* 302
Acupuncture/acupressure
  techniques
  A *1:* 202–04
Acupuncture and Daoism
  PS 161
Adam and Eve
  A *1:* 220 (ill.)
Adi Granth. *See* Granth Sahib
Adur Aduran
  A *2:* 454
Advaita Vedanta school
  B *2:* 239, 240, 385–86
  See also Upanishads
Advent
  A *1:* 140
Adventist doctrines
  A *1:* 130
Aeneid (Virgil)
  A *1:* 211, 224, 228
Aeschylus
  A *1:* 211
Aesir class
  A *2:* 377

Afghanistan, destruction of sacred
    art in
    A *1:* 114
Africa, Mother Goddess in
    A *1:* 7
African Americans, Islam and
    A *2:* 300
African communities,
    cultural roles in
    B *2:* 346
African indigenous religions
    belief in supreme God
    A *2:* 276
    overview
    A *2:* 275
Africans, influence on Vodou
    A *2:* 80
Afrinagen ritual
    A *2:* 456–57
Afterlife
    A *1:* 47, 135–36
Agami Karma
    A *2:* 263
Age of Enlightenment
    A *1:* 25–26
"Agnosticism" (Huxley)
    A *1:* 32
Agnosticism and Atheism
    A *1:* **19–36**
    about
    A *1:* 22
    agnosticism
    A *1:* 28
    described
    A *1:* 19
    weak *versus* strong
    A *1:* 30–31
    See also Huxley,
        Thomas Henry
"Agnosticism and Christianity"
    (Huxley)
    PS 4
Agnostics, about
    PS 4
Agnostics, number of
    A *1:* 20

Ahimsa
    B *2:* 246
    PS 137, 140
Ahimsa vow
    A *2:* 323
Ahriman
    PS 189
Ahunavaiti Gatha
    PS 186, 189–90
Ahura Mazda
    A *2:* 443, 448 (ill.), 451
Aisha (widow of Muhammad)
    B *1:* 30; *2:* 304
Aiwisruthrem
    A *2:* 456
Ajiva
    A *2:* 330
Akaranga Sutra
    A *2:* 327, 334
    PS 121, 137, 138
Akh soul
    A *1:* 47
Akhand Paath ceremony
    A *2:* 435
Akhenaten
    A *1:* 44–45, 45–46
    B *1:* **9–16,** 9 (ill.),
        13 (ill.)
    life of
    B *1:* 10
    reign of
    B *1:* 11, 14
Akhenaton. *See* Akhenaten
Akhetaten (city)
    B *1:* 12, 15 (ill.)
Akkad (city)
    B *1:* 123
Akkadians
    A *1:* 40–41
    B *1:* 123
Aktiu festival
    A *1:* 57
Al-Amin. *See* Muhammad
Albert Schweitzer International
    Prize
    B *2:* 294

Alchemy and Daoism
    A *1:* 180
Alcohol abstinance
    A *1:* 110
Al-Din, Salah. *See* Saladin
Aleinu prayer
    A *2:* 361
Aleph
    A *2:* 401
Alexander the Great
    A *1:* 211, 217; *2:* 447
    B *1:* 36 (ill.); *2:* 405
    PS 187
    See also Aristotle
Alexandria, Egypt, library of
    A *1:* 217
Ali, Hussain, Ibn
    A *2:* 298
ʿAli, Muhammad
    A *1:* 73, 76
Ali (caliph)
    A *2:* 298
ʿAli Abī Ibn Tālib
    B *1:* **17–24**
    death of
    B *1:* 22
    early life
    B *1:* 18
    fourth caliph
    B *1:* 21–22
    Muhammad and
    B *1:* 19, 200
    succession issue
    B *1:* 17–18
"Ali Baba and the Forty
    Thieves,"
    A *2:* 320
Ali ibn Abi Talib, Hazrat
    A *2:* 301
ʿAli Muhammad, Siyyid
    B *1:* 44
Ali Muhammad of Shiraz,
    Sayyid. *See* Bab
All Hallows' Day
    A *2:* 390
All Saints Day
    A *2:* 390

Allah
    A *2:* 304–05
Allah's name
    PS 28 (ill.)
"Allegory of the Cave" (Plato)
    A *1:* 229
    B *2:* 317–18
Almohads, conquest of Spain
    B *2:* 250
Al-Qaeda group
    A *2:* 321
Am I An Atheist or An Agnostic?
    (Russell)
    A *1:* 33
Ama-no-Nuboko
    PS 17
Amar Das, Guru
    A *2:* 421
    PS 86
Amarna period
    B *1:* 11, 15
Amaterasu (goddess)
    A *2:* 395, 397 (ill.),
        402, 406–07
    PS 3, 15, 20–21
Amenhotep IV. *See* Akhenaten
Ame-no-Minaka-Nushi-no-
    Mikoto
    PS 16
Amen-Ra (sun god)
    A *1:* 38, 42, 44, 45, 61
Ameretat
    A *2:* 451
Ameretat concept
    PS 186
America, spread of Islam in
    A *2:* 300
America Israelite newspaper
    B *2:* 395
American Association for the
    Advancement of Atheism
    PS 200
American Atheists, Inc.
    PS 201
American Baptist Convention
    A *1:* 134

American Indians
    (North America)
    A *2:* 271
Amesha Spentas
    A *2:* 451
    PS 186–87
Amidah prayer
    A *2:* 359
Ammut (goddess)
    A *1:* 48
Amram
    B *2:* 279
Amrit ritual
    A *2:* 427
    See also Khanda symbol.
Amrit Sanskar ceremony
    A *2:* 434, 435
Amritsar (city)
    A *2:* 436–37
An/Anu (sky god)
    A *1:* 37, 47
    B *1:* 122
An Quang Buddhist Institute
    B *2:* 360
Anabaptists
    A *1:* 134
Anagarika Dharmapala
    A *1:* 93
Analects (Confucius)
    A *1:* 155, 164
    B *1:* 88, 89
The Analects of Confucius
    PS 125–36
    Book 1
    PS 130–33, 133–35
    Book 2
    PS 128, 129
    Book 10
    PS 126
    Book 12
    PS 126
    overview
    PS 125–26
    style of
    PS 129
Anandatirtha. *See* Madhva

Anandpur, Battle of
    B *2:* 355
Anandpur siege
    B *2:* 356
Anarchist, defined
    PS 193
Anaxagoras
    A *1:* 24, 215
    B *1:* **25–31,** 25 (ill.)
    early life
    B *1:* 25–26
    exile of
    B *1:* 29
    theories of
    B *1:* 27–28
Anaximander
    A *1:* 213, 237
    B *1:* 26
Anaximenes
    A *1:* 213
    B *1:* 26–27
Ancestor worship
    A *1:* 6, 6 (ill.), 166, 172,
        183; *2:* 284
Ancestral spirits
    A *2:* 281, 402
Ancient Egypt and
    Mesopotamia (ill.)
    A *1:* 43
Ancient Order of Druids
    A *2:* 381–82
Ancient Religions of Egypt
    and Mesopotamia
    A *1:* **37–67**
Andrew (apostle/disciple)
    A *1:* 121
Anga scripture group
    A *2:* 333–34
Angabaha scripture group
    A *2:* 333
Angad, Guru
    A *2:* 421
Angad Dev, Guru
    PS 86
Angel of Death
    PS 24

Angels, belief in
  PS 23–24
Angkor Wat temple
  A *1:* 106
Anglican Church/Church
  of England
  A *1:* 134
"Anglo-Sikh Wars"
  A *2:* 423
Angra Mainyu
  A *2:* 443, 447, 451–52
  PS 189
Angra Mainyu spirit
  B *2:* 402
Angulimala Paritta prayer
  A *1:* 111
Anicca principle of Buddhism
  A *1:* 98–99
Animal sacrifices, in Santería
  A *2:* 283–84
Animals, worship of
  A *1:* 42
Anime
  A *2:* 416
Anjali mudra
  A *1:* 109; *2:* 265
Ankh symbol, gods seen with
  A *1:* 51
Ano San, Mount
  A *2:* 413
Anselm of Canterbury
  A *1:* 25
Anthesteria festival
  A *1:* 231
Anthropologists, view of
  religion by
  A *1:* 4
Antigone (Sophocles)
  A *1:* 211
Antioch incident
  B *2:* 306
Antiochus IV
  A *2:* 364
Anti-Semitism
  B *2:* 212, 275
Anu (god)

A *1:* 40, 61
Anubis (god)
  A *1:* 43, 48, 61
Anuradhpura temple complex
  (Sri Lanka)
  A *1:* 110
Apache tribe
  A *2:* 288–89
Aparigraha vow
  A *2:* 323
  B *2:* 246
Apartheid
  B *2:* 367–68, 370–71
Apathia described
  A *1:* 218
Apeiron
  A *1:* 213
Aphrodite (goddess)
  A *1:* 7, 221
Apollo (god)
  A *1:* 122, 222, 230
Apologia (Plato)
  B *2:* 314, 315
Apostle
  B *1:* 3
Apostles of Jesus Christ.
  See individual apostles
Aquinas, Thomas
  A *1:* 25, 147, 237
Arabian Nights
  A *2:* 319–20
Arafat, Mount
  B *1:* 198 (ill.)
Aranyakas (theologies)
  A *2:* 251
Arawak Indians
  A *2:* 280
Arawn
  A *2:* 380
Arche
  A *1:* 213
Architecture
  Buddhist influence on
  A *1:* 115
  Christian influence on
  A *1:* 148

Muslim contributions to
  A *2:* 318–19
Ardechir I
  A *2:* 448 (ill.)
Ardha Magadhi language
  A *2:* 334
Ares (god)
  A *1:* 221
Arihant concept
  A *2:* 332
Aristocles. *See* Plato
Aristotle
  A *1:* 217, 217 (ill.), 218, 226
  B *1:* **33–40,** 33 (ill.), 36 (ill.)
  described
  B *1:* 38
  education
  B *1:* 34–35
  intellectual growth of
  B *1:* 35–36
  teachings
  B *1:* 37
  Western intellectual study and
  B *1:* 34
  works of
  B *1:* 38–40
  See also Plato
Arjan Dev (Guru)
  A *2:* 422, 437
  B *1:* 155
  PS 86
Arjuna. *See Mahabharata*
Ark of the Covenant
  A *2:* 346
  See also Ten Commandments
Arkan al Islami (Pillars of Islam)
  A *2:* 305–06
Armit ceremony
  B *1:* 158
Art
  Muslim contributions to
  A *2:* 317–18
  under rule of Akhenaten
  A *1:* 66
Art in ancient Egypt
  B *1:* 11, 12, 13 (ill.)

Artemis (goddess)
   A *1:* 7, 222, 230
Artha
   A *2:* 248
Arthasastra
   A *2:* 265
Artifacts, use of in indigenous
   religions
   A *2:* 273
Artisan class, in ancient Egypt
   A *1:* 62
Arts, Jewish influence on
   A *2:* 369
Arya Samaj sect
   B *1:* 104–05
Asatru (god)
   A *2:* 377 (ill.)
   PS 97
   followers of
   A *2:* 374
   origins of
   A *2:* 376–77
   symbols of
   A *2:* 378
Ascension of Abdu'l-Baha holiday
   A *1:* 82
Ascension of Bahá'u'lláh
   holiday
   A *1:* 82
Ash Wednesday
   A *1:* 141
Asha defined
   PS 186–87, 189
Asha Vahishta
   A *2:* 451
Asha Vahishta concept
   PS 186
Asher (son of Jacob)
   B *1:* 6
Ashkenazic Jews
   A *2:* 350
Ashoka of Maurya (emperor)
   A *1:* 91–92, 109–10
Ashramas
   A *2:* 248
Ashtur (god), cult of

A *1:* 45
Asia, Buddhism in
   A *1:* 92
Asoka. *See* Ashoka of
   Maurya (emperor)
Asparigrah vow
   PS 138
Assassins
   A *2:* 299
   B *1:* 146 (ill.), 148
Asteya vow
   A *2:* 323
   B *2:* 246
   PS 137
Astrology, in Babylonia
   A *1:* 41, 55
Ataraxia, in Stoicism
   A *1:* 218
Atash Bahram symbol
   A *2:* 454
Aten (god)
   A *1:* 44
Atenism
   A *1:* 45–46
   B *1:* 12
Atharva Veda
   A *2:* 251
Atheism
   A *1:* 27 (ill.)
   about
   A *1:* 21–22
   categories of
   A *1:* 30
   defined
   PS 195–96
   described
   A *1:* 19
   development of in China
   A *1:* 22
   Greek rationalists and
   A *1:* 237
   moral basis for
   PS 123
   negative meaning of
   A *1:* 26
   number of atheists
   A *1:* 20–21

and science
   PS 201
   state-sponsored
   A *1:* 29–30
   weak *versus* strong
   PS 194
   *See also On the Nature
   of Things* (Lucretius);
   Religious atheism;
   Anaxagoras; Marx, Karl
Atheists
   PS 4, 193
Atheists United
   PS 201
Athena (goddess)
   A *1:* 221–22, 223, 230
Atmaramji
   A *2:* 328
Atomic theory
   A *1:* 237
Atomists
   A *1:* 24, 215
Atoms
   A *1:* 215 (ill.)
Atonement
   A *1:* 135
Atrakhasis Babylonian epic
   PS 11
Atum (god)
   A *1:* 43
Augurs
   A *1:* 231
Augustine of Hippo
   A *1:* 25
Aum
   A *2:* 287
Aum Shinrikyo
   A *2:* 401
Aum symbol
   A *2:* 253–54
Aurangzeb
   B *2:* 351, 356
Auspicious days, in Hinduism
   A *2:* 260
Australian, Mother Goddess in
   A *1:* 7

Autumn Festival
  A *2:* 411
Autumn Remembering
  A *1:* 167
Avalokitesvara
  A *1:* 103
Avesta
  A *2:* 453
  B *2:* 400, 401
  PS 122, 188
  See also The Gathas
Avesta as reproduced in *The Divine Sons of Zarathushtra*
  PS 185–92
Avestan language
  A *2:* 453
  PS 188
Avidya, explained
  PS 166
Awen symbol
  A *2:* 381
Ay
  B *1:* 10
Ayat. See Qur'an
Ayathrem festival
  A *2:* 458
Ayatul Kursi
  A *2:* 304
Ayurveda
  A *2:* 268
Azal, Subh-i
  A *1:* 71, 72
Azalis. *See* Yahya, Mirza
Azan
  A *2:* 312
Azra'il (angel)
  PS 24
Azrail
  A *2:* 309
Aztec religion
  A *2:* 274 (ill.)

B

Ba soul
  A *1:* 47

Baal Shem Tov. *See* Ben Eliezer, Israel
Bab
  A *1:* 69–70
  PS 176–77
  See also 'Ali Muhammad, Siyyid
Bab birthday holiday
  A *1:* 82
Baba Dayal
  A *2:* 426
Babalz Ayi (orisha), renaming of
  A *2:* 283
Babi faith
  A *1:* 69–70
Babis, massacre of
  A *1:* 71
Babism
  B *1:* 44
Babylonia, idol worship in
  B *1:* 2
Babylonian Genesis
  PS 11
Babylonian Talmud. *See* Talmud
Babylonians, changes to religion by
  A *1:* 41
Babylonians, supreme being in creation stories of
  PS 3
Bacchanalia
  A *1:* 226
Bacchus
  A *1:* 122, 226
Bach, Johann Sebastian
  A *1:* 148
Bacon, Francis
  PS 195
Bactria
  A *2:* 447
  B *2:* 403
Bactria, Zarathushtra in
  PS 191
Badr, Battle of
  B *1:* 19
Bagua (pa hua) symbol
  A *1:* 192

Bahá'í
  A *1:* **69–86,** 72 (ill.)
  central belief of
  A *1:* 77, 84
  essential elements of
  PS 178
  fasting and
  A *1:* 79
  followers of
  A *1:* 73
  growth of
  A *1:* 74
  history of
  A *1:* 69
  holy days of
  A *1:* 81–82
  moral basis of
  PS 122–23
  overview of
  PS 175
  persecution of members of
  A *1:* 75
  PS 183
  prayers and tithing
  A *1:* 83
  sacred numbers of
  A *1:* 70, 80
  social action and
  PS 178
  structure of
  A *1:* 80–81
  symbols of
  A *1:* 80
  twelve principles of
  B *1:* 44
  United Nations and
  A *1:* 84
  PS 178
  See also Sermon on the Mount
Bahá'í's temple
  B *1:* 42 (ill.)
Bahá'u'lláh
  B *1:* **41–49**
  banishment of
  A *1:* 72
  birthday holiday

A *1:* 82
death of
A *1:* 73
B *1:* 48
imprisonment
B *1:* 47
life and writings of
PS 176–77
movements in exile
B *1:* 47 (ill.)
poisoning
B *1:* 46–47
self-exile of
A *1:* 71
successors to
A *1:* 73–74
view of in Bahá'í
A *1:* 4
vision of
A *1:* 71
See also Nuri,
    Mirza Husayn 'Ali
Bahubali statue
A *2:* 329
Baisakhi holiday
A *2:* 435
Bala Barua, Nani. *See* Dipa Ma
Balance principle
  A *1:* 220; *2:* 383
Balfour Declaration
A *2:* 248
Balthasar (magi)
B *2:* 403
Balzan Prize
B *2:* 354
Bamiyan, Afghanistan,
  destruction of Buddha
  Vairocana
A *1:* 114
Banda Singh Bahadur
A *2:* 423
Bandi Chhor holiday
A *2:* 436
Bani Hashim clan
B *1:* 18
Bantu Education Act

B *2:* 369
Baor initiation
B *2:* 346–47
Baptism, in Christian church
A *1:* 124, 138, 142–43,
    142 (ill.)
Baptist Church
A *1:* 134
Bar Mitzvah
A *2:* 366
Bardo period, in Buddhism
A *1:* 114
Bards class in Druidism
A *2:* 379
Barquq
B *1:* 168
Basra
B *1:* 12
Basri, Hasan Al-
B *2:* 322
Basri, Rabi'a Al-.
  See Rābi'a al-Adawiyah
Bat Mitzvah
A *2:* 366
Battle of Tours
A *2:* 294
Bauer, Bruno
B *2:* 258–59
Bayan (Bahá'u'lláh)
B *1:* 53
Bayan Wujub al-Hijra
  (Usuman Dan Fodio)
B *2:* 379
Bayanis. *See* Yahya, Mirza
Beatification
B *2:* 356
Beatitudes
PS 212
Bedouins
B *1:* 166–67, 194
Behavior, code of
A *1:* 1
Behavior, guidance for
PS 126
Behdin. *See* Zoroastrianism
Behdini

A *2:* 443
Behramshah Shroff
A *2:* 449
Beindriya beings
A *2:* 331
Beliefs, common elements of
PS 123
Bell
A *2:* 388
Beltane (Beltaine) Sabbat
A *2:* 389
Beltaine (Bealteinne) festival
A *2:* 381
Ben Eliezer, Israel
A *2:* 351
B *1:* 171–78
early life
B *1:* 172–74
followers
B *1:* 177
spiritual awakening
B *1:* 174–77
Ben Maimon, Moshe
A *2:* 352, 354
Benedictine Order
A *1:* 126
Benedictine Rule
A *1:* 126
Benjamin (son of Jacob)
B *1:* 6
Berbers
B *1:* 166
Bereshit
PS 5
Bernhard, Isaac
B *2:* 268–69
Besht. *See* Ben Eliezer, Israel
Beth Jeshurun (Yeshurun)
B *2:* 393
Bethel
B *1:* 3
Bethlehem, pilgrimages to
A *1:* 141
Bhagavad Gita
A *2:* 244, 252–53
PS 110

Bhagavad Purana
  B *2:* 331
Bhai Mani Singh
  A *2:* 430
Bhakti (devotion)
  A *2:* 256
Bhakti movement
  B *2:* 333–40
Bhakti yoga
  A *2:* 250
Bhikkhu
  B *1:* 64
Bhikkhuni
  B *1:* 64
Bhutto, Benazir
  A *2:* 320
Bhyadrabhanuswami
  A *2:* 333
Bible
  A *1:* 34, 136–37; *2:* 368–69
  PS 203–12
  about
  PS 203
  arrangement of
  PS 205
  translations of
  PS 211–12
Bidayat al-Hidayah
  (The Beginning of Guidance)
  (al-Ghazālī)
  B *1:* 149
"Big five" religions
  A *1:* 8
Bile/Bel/Belenus (god)
  A *2:* 380
Bill, Buffalo
  B *1:* 54–55
Biology, classification systems and
  A *1:* 237
The Birth of Venus (Botticelli)
  A *1:* 236
Birth rituals
  Buddhist
  A *1:* 111
  Confucian
  A *1:* 170

Egyptian
  A *1:* 63
Mesopotamian
  A *1:* 60
Roman
  A *1:* 235
Black Elk
  B *1:* **51–58,** 51 (ill.)
  PS 39 (ill.)
  early years of
  PS 33–34
  great vision of
  PS 34–36
  visions of
  B *1:* 52–53, 55
  See also Foundation Myths;
    Ghost Dance
Black Elk, Nicholas.
  See Black Elk
***Black Elk Speaks: Being the
  Life Story of a Holy Man of
  the Oglala Sioux*** (Neihardt)
  B *1:* 52, 57
  PS 33–43
  as foundation myth
  PS 34
  six grandfathers in
  PS 34–35
  symbols in
  PS 35–36
Blavatsky, Helena
  B *1:* 108–09, 130
Blim Chand
  B *1:* 155
Bloch, Therese
  B *2:* 392
Blockages, removing
  A *1:* 187–88
Blot ritual
  A *2:* 378
Bodh Gaya, pilgrimages to
  A *1:* 108
Bodhi tree symbol
  A *1:* 101–02
Bodhisattvas
  B *1:* 65

Bodhisattvas, recognition of
  A *1:* 95, 99
Boer War
  B *1:* 132
Bojaxhiu, Agnes Gonxha.
  See Teresa, Mother
Bon religion
  A *2:* 289–90
Bonnet, Charles
  B *2:* 271, 277
Book of Abraham
  B *1:* 4 (ill.)
The Book of Amdurat
  A *1:* 48
The Book of Caverns
  A *1:* 48
The Book of Certitude
  A *1:* 71
  B *1:* 45
Book of Changes (Confucius)
  A *1:* 164
  PS 136
Book of Fatima
  PS 182–83
The Book of Gates
  A *1:* 48
Book of Judith
  A *2:* 368–69
*The Book of One Thousand and
  One Nights*
  A *2:* 319–20
Book of Shadows
  A *2:* 388
  B *1:* 140
The Book of the Dead
  A *1:* 48, 49–51, 50 (ill.)
"The Book of the Way and
  Its Virtue." *See* Dao De Jing
"Book of Zhuang"
  A *1:* 178
Bounteous Immortals
  PS 186
Boycott of South Africa
  B *2:* 371
Brahma (Brahman)
  A *2:* 246–47, 262

PS 111 (ill.), 119
See also Aum symbol
Brahmacharya stage
  A *2:* 248
Brahmacharya vow
  A *2:* 323
  B *2:* 246
  PS 138
Brahmanas (rituals)
  A *2:* 25
Brahmins (caste)
  A *2:* 263
Brahmo Samaj movement
  B *2:* 384–85
Bridal rituals in Rome
  A *1:* 235
Brigid/Brigit (goddess)
  A *2:* 379, 380
Brihadaranyaka Upanishad
  A *2:* 252
Brings White, Anne
  B *1:* 56
British Buddhist
  B *1:* 112
British Circle of Universal Bond
  A *2:* 382
British Druid Order
  A *2:* 382
Brooms
  A *2:* 387
Brooms, as sacred tools
  PS 101, 104 (ill.)
Buchenwald concentration camp
  B *2:* 364
Buckley, Raymond
  B *1:* 142
The Buddha
  B *1:* **59–66,** 59 (ill.), 61 (ill.)
  PS 168 (ill.)
  birth of
  A *1:* 98 (ill.)
  death of
  A *1:* 90
  depictions of
  A *1:* 114–15

early life
  B *1:* 59–60
spiritual quest of
  B *1:* 60–61
teachings of
  A *1:* 23
  B *1:* 107
See also Buddhism;
  Eightfold Path
Buddha Amitabha
  A *1:* 95
*Buddha Heart, Buddha Mind:
  Living the Four Noble Truths*
  (Dalai Lama)
  B *1:* 97
Buddha Vairocana
  A *1:* 114
Buddhahood
  B *2:* 296
Buddha-nature
  B *2:* 294
Buddha-nature, realizing
  A *1:* 100
Buddhism
  A *1:* **87–117**
  about
  A *1:* 91
  basic principles of
  A *1:* 96–99
  central beliefs of
  A *1:* 90, 98–99
  creator-god concept and
  A *1:* 19, 23
  daily practice of
  A *1:* 110–11
  decline of in India
  A *1:* 92
  disagreements within
  A *1:* 90
  form of worship
  A *1:* 102–03
  growth of
  A *1:* 92–94, 93 (ill.)
  holy days in
  A *1:* 106–08
  influence on art of

A *1:* 115
in Japan
  B *2:* 296–99
main types of
  A *1:* 94–95
major branches of
  B *2:* 297–98
moral basis for
  PS 122
practice techniques of
  A *1:* 95
overview
  A *1:* 87
rise of
  A *1:* 8
symbols of
  A *1:* 101–02
texts of
  PS 167
two schools of
  B *1:* 65–66
  PS 172
in Vietnam
  B *2:* 362
Buddhist flag
  A *1:* 102
Buddhist monks
  B *2:* 364 (ill.)
Buddhist nuns
  B *1:* 64, 118 (ill.)
Buffalo Bill's Wild West Show
  B *1:* 54–55
Buffalo/bison
  A *2:* 287, 288
Bulla charm
  A *1:* 235
Bundahism
  B *2:* 401
Buraq (winged horse)
  B *2:* 289, 303
Bure, Idelette De
  B *1:* 78
Burkina Faso
  B *2:* 368, 379
Burma (Myanmar)
  A *1:* 94

Bushido code
A *1:* 173
Bushmen of Africa, creation/
foundation myths of
PS 3
Buzurg, Mirza
B *1:* 41
Byzantine Empire
A *1:* 127

C

Cairo, Eqypt
B *1:* 168
Caitanya Mahaprabhu
A *2:* 244
B *1:* **67–73,** 68 (ill.)
early life
B *1:* 68–69
miracles
B *1:* 70–71
writings
B *1:* 70
Caitanyas
A *2:* 244–45, 249 (ill.)
Calendars
A *1:* 140; *2:* 457
Calf Pipe
A *2:* 288
Calligraphy
A *1:* 115, 204; *2:* 303 (ill.)
Calvin, John
A *1:* 133
B *1:* **75–82,** 75 (ill.), 81 (ill.)
conversion
B *1:* 76
early life
B *1:* 76–77
influence
B *1:* 80–81
Calvinism
B *1:* 75, 78
See also Predestination
Cambodia
A *1:* 92, 94

Cambyses II
A *2:* 450
Camel, Battle of the
B *1:* 22
Canaan, Mother Goddess in
A *1:* 7
Canaanites
B *1:* 3
Candide (Voltaire)
B *2:* 269, 275
Candomblé
A *2:* 280, 282
Canterbury Tales (Chaucer)
A *1:* 147
Cao Guojin (god)
A *1:* 190
Capitalism
B *2:* 259, 265
Caravans
B *1:* 196
Carchemish
A *1:* 6
Carolis, H. Don
B *1:* 107
Carter, Howard
B *1:* 14
Carvaka, concept of creator-god
and
A *1:* 23
Caspar (magi)
B *2:* 403
Caste system
B *1:* 70–71; *2:* 235–36,
248, 385
PS 85
creation of
A *2:* 242
Indian constitution and
A *2:* 263–64
Jains and
A *2:* 340
Sikhism and
A *2:* 421
Çatalhöyük
A *1:* 6
The Catastrophe of Eger (Wise)

B *2:* 397
Catholic/Protestant conflicts
B *2:* 231–32
Cauldron
A *2:* 388
Cauvin, Jean. *See* Calvin, John
Celestial Masters
A *1:* 179, 183, 198
Celts
A *2:* 373–74, 379
Censer
A *2:* 388
Central Conference of American
Rabbis
B *2:* 391, 394, 396
Central Institute of Higher
Tibetan Studies
B *1:* 96
Ceremony, importance of in
Confucianism
A *1:* 162
Ceres
A *1:* 122
Cerridwen
A *2:* 380
Ceylon, religious changes in
B *1:* 108
Ch'an Buddhism
A *1:* 95
See also Zen Buddhism
Chagall, Marc
A *2:* 369
Chakkar symbol
A *2:* 432
Chamkaur, Battle of
B *2:* 356
Chandragiri hill
A *2:* 339
Change, nature of
A *1:* 227
Chanting meditation technique
A *1:* 104
Charaka
A *2:* 265
Charles I
B *2:* 231

Charmides (Plato)
  B *2:* 315
Charming of the Plow holiday
  A *2:* 378
Chathurveda
  A *2:* 251
Chaucer, Geoffrey
  A *1:* 147
Chaurindriya beings
  A *2:* 331
Chiang Kai-shek
  A *1:* 181–82
Chih-i
  B *2:* 312
China
  Buddhism in
  A *1:* 92
  non-believers in
  A *1:* 31
  religious tradition in
  A *1:* 95
  Western influences on
    religion of
  A *1:* 159
China, during the time of
  Confucius
  B *1:* 84
Chinese art, close observation
  and
  A *1:* 204
Chinese communists, effect on
  Daoism
  PS 161
Chinese history, Spring
  and Autumn Period of
  A *1:* 154
Chinese landscape painting
  A *1:* 174
Chinese language, Daoism and
  A *1:* 205
Chinese literature, Daoism and
  A *1:* 204–05
Chinese New Year festival
  A *1:* 167, 168, 196–97
Chinese texts, translating
  PS 129

Ching Ming festival
  A *1:* 167, 168
Chong Son
  A *1:* 174
Christian Church,
  separation of
  A *1:* 127
Christian creation concepts
  A *1:* 28
Christian Crusaders, Jews in
  Europe and
  A *2:* 348
Christian Evidences (Bonnet)
  B *2:* 277
Christian gospels
  A *1:* 124
Christianity
  A *1:* **119–49**
  B *1:* 190–91, 192–93
  about
  A *1:* 122
  adaptions of from Judaism
  A *1:* 123–24
  basic beliefs of
  A *1:* 134–35
  beginnings of
  A *1:* 123
  buracracy of
  A *1:* 125
  doctrines of
  A *1:* 135–36
  forms of worship service
  A *1:* 139
  Gospels of
  A *1:* 124
  Greek and Roman
    influences on
  A *1:* 136
  influence of
    Zoroastrianism on
  A *2:* 452
  PS 188
  influences of
  A *1:* 146–48
  and Islam

· **A** *1:* 127–28
  Judaism and
  PS 204–05
  language of worship of
  A *1:* 126–27
  moral basis for
  PS 122
  missionaries of
  A *1:* 125
  and Neoplatonism
  A *1:* 219
  observances of
  A *1:* 140
  overview
  A *1:* 119
  rise of
  A *1:* 8
  sacraments of
  A *1:* 124
  schisms in
  A *1:* 130–31
  similarity of Zoroastrianism to
  PS 191–92
  spread of
  A *1:* 123, 124 (ill.), 125
  supreme being in creation
    accounts of
  PS 3
  symbols of
  A *1:* 137–38, 137 (ill.)
  worship language of
  A *1:* 126
  See also Jesus Christ
Christians
  number of
  A *1:* 2
  persecution of
  A *1:* 125
Christmas
  A *1:* 15, 140
Chronos
  A *1:* 223
Chrysippus
  A *1:* 218
Chu Hsi
  A *1:* 157

Chuang-tzu
  A *1:* 178
Chung Yeung Festival
  A *1:* 167
Chunqiu (Ch'un-ch'iu)
  A *1:* 164
Church of England/Anglican
  Church
  A *1:* 134
Church of Jesus Christ of Latter-
  day Saints
  A *1:*134
Church of Martin Luther
  A *1:* 141
Church of the Holy
  Sepulcher (tomb)
  A *1:* 141
Circle symbol
  A *2:* 287–88
Cities and city-states,
  in Mesopotamia
  A *1:* 39, 59
City states
  B *2:* 313
"Civil Disobedience" (Thoreau)
  B *1:* 130
Civilization, cyclical nature of
  B *1:* 166–67
Classic of Documents
  (Confucius)
  A *1:* 164
  PS 136
Classic of Filial Piety
  A *1:* 164
Classic of Odes (Confucius)
  A *1:* 164
  PS 136
"Classic of the Great Peace"
  A *1:* 191
Cleanliness
  PS 30
Clement VI (pope)
  B *2:* 227
Clergy, clothing of
  A *1:* 142
Clutterbuck, Dorothy

B *1:* 139–40
Collected Essays vol. 5: *Science
  and Christian Tradition*
  PS 45–54
Cologne Cathedral
  A *1:* 141
Cologne Circle
  B *2:* 265
Columbian Exposition in
  Chicago
  PS 112
Communism
  A *1:* 21, 29–30, 130
  B *2:* 265
Communist Correspondence
  Committee
  B *2:* 266
Communist League
  B *2:* 266
The Communist Manifesto
  (Marx; Engles)
  B *2:* 267
Community of believers
  A *1:* 11; *2:* 274–75
Community participation,
  in indigenous religions
  A *2:* 273
Compassion, in Daoism
  A *1:* 187
Complete Perfection sect
  A *1:* 185
Confession sacrament
  A *1:* 145–46
Confirmation sacrament
  A *1:* 138, 143
Confucian Classics
  A *1:* 156
Confucian philosophy
  goals
  B *1:* 86–88
  main principle
  B *1:* 83–84
Confucian temple
  B *1:* 86 (ill.)
Confucian Temple of Literature
  A *1:* 166

Confucianism
  A *1:* **151–76,** 165 (ill.),
    170 (ill.)
  about
  A *1:* 156
  after death of Confucius
  A *1:* 155–56
  ban on
  PS 135
  belief system of
  A *1:* 168
  and concept of creator-god
  A *1:* 22
  development of principles of
  A *1:* 153
  influence on education
  A *1:* 175
  in Japan and Korea
  A *1:* 160
  moral basis for
  PS 121
  number of followers
  A *1:* 152
  pilgrimages
  A *1:* 169
  political guidance of
  PS 128
  rise of
  A *1:* 8
  rites of
  A *1:* 170
  spiritual elements of
  A *1:* 156–57
  spread of
  A *1:* 158–59
  as state religion
  A *1:* 156
  suppression of
  A *1:* 159
  See also De (te) principle;
    Junzi (chun-tze) principle;
    Ren principle;
    Wen principle
Confucius
  A *1:* 158 (ill.)
  B *1:* **83–90,** 83 (ill.)

about
PS 125, 126–28
beliefs
B *1:* 85–87
early life
B *1:* 85
education of
PS 130
exile
B *1:* 88
as government reformer
A *1:* 154
life of
A *1:* 153
social class of
PS 129–30
teaching method of
A *1:* 155
writings of
A *1:* 170
PS 136
Confucius Culture Festival
PS 131 (ill.)
Congregations of Israel
B *1:* 176
Congress Party
B *1:* 134
Congressional Gold Medal
B *2:* 355
Connectedness, emphasis on in
Daoism
PS 150
Conservative Judaism
A *2:* 352
B *2:* 394
Constantine (emperor)
A *1:* 125, 128 (ill.), 212
*Contribution to the Critique of
Hegel's Philosophy of Law* (Marx)
A *1:* 32
Conversions of West Africans
B *2:* 368
The Convert (Wise)
B *2:* 397
Cop, Nicholas
B *1:* 76–77

Córdoba (Spain), caliphate at
A *2:* 298
Corinth
A *1:* 223
Corpus Christi Movement
B *2:* 294, 354
The Cosmic God (Wise)
B *2:* 397
Cosmos, nature of
A *1:* 22
Council for a Parliament of the
World's Religions
PS 119
Council of Jerusalem
B *2:* 305–06
Counter-Reformation
A *1:* 129
Coven initiation
A *2:* 388
Covenant breaker
A *1:* 76
"Covenant" concept
A *2:* 355
PS 10
Covens, defined
PS 106
Co-Workers of Mother Teresa
B *2:* 294, 354
Cows, sacred nature of
A *2:* 253
Cratylus (Plato)
B *2:* 316
Crazy Horse
B *1:* 53–54
Creation, male and female
principles in
PS 14
Creation myths
A *1:* 226
PS 1
ancient Egypt
A *1:* 43
Greece
A *1:* 223
Japan
A *2:* 405–06

Rome
A 1: 224
See also Ra/Re (sun god)
Creation of mandalas, in
Vajrayana Buddhism
A *1:* 95
Creation stories
PS 1–4
Fulani people
PS 2
location from which creation
began
PS 3–4
themes of
PS 2–4
See also Agnostics; Atheism;
Bereshit; *specific creation
stories*
Creator-god
A *1:* 19, 23, 126
PS 6, 86
Cremation
A *1:* 113
Crete, Mother Goddess worship in
A *1:* 7
Critias (Plato)
B *2:* 317, 331
Critique of Pure Reason (Kant)
A *1:* 26
*Critique of the Helgelian
Philosophy of Public Law* (Marx)
B *2:* 264, 270
The Crito (Plato)
B *2:* 315
Cross symbol
A *1:* 137
Crowley, Aleister
B *1:* 140
Crusades
A *1:* 127–28; *2:* 299
Crystal sphere
A *2:* 388
Cuba, Vodou in
A *2:* 280
Cults
Ashur

A *1:* 10
Marduk
A *1:* 45
meanings of
A *1:* 10
Cultural Revolution
A *1:* 182
Cuneiform writing system
A *1:* 65
Cunningham, Scott
PS 97
Cupid, symbols of
A *1:* 230
Cybele (goddess)
A *1:* 7, 220
Cycle of life. *See* Karma
Cyprus
B *1:* 138–39
Cyrus of Persia
A *1:* 41
Czolgosz, Leon
PS 201

D

Da Vinci, Leonardo
A *1:* 147–48
Da Xue (Ta Hsueh)
A *1:* 163
Dacheng Dia
A *1:* 169
Daevas
A *2:* 446–47, 451
PS 189
Dagara tribe
B *2:* 349
Dagpa (god)
A *2:* 289
Dahomean tribes
A *2:* 280–81
Dakota tribe
A *2:* 287–88
Dalai Lama
A *1:* 92
B *1:* **91–99,** 91 (ill.)

early life
B *1:* 92–93
exile
B *1:* 95–98
religious training
B *1:* 93
response to Chinese invasion
of Tibet
B *1:* 94–95
travels
B *1:* 97–98
Damascus
B *1:* 3
Damascus, capture of
A *2:* 298
Dan (son of Jacob)
B *1:* 6
Dan (Tan). *See* Laozi
Dana, Charles
B *2:* 262, 268
Dana (generosity)
A *1:* 104–05,
105 (ill.)
Danishmends
A *2:* 299
Dante Alighieri
A *1:* 147
Danu
A *2:* 380
Dao character symbol
A *1:* 192
Dao De Jing (Laozi)
A *1:* 31, 189
B *2:* 206, 207
PS 122, **149–63**
central beliefs of
PS 150
compilation of
PS 154
overview of
PS 149
themes of
PS 152
translation of
PS 152–53
writing style of

PS 153
Dao jiao. *See* Religious Daoism
Daoism
A *1:* **177–206**
B *2:* 207–08
about
A *1:* 180
compared to other religions
PS 150
Confucianism and
PS 135
creator-god concept and
A *1:* 19, 31
in daily life
A *1:* 201
decline of
PS 160–61
divisions in
A *1:* 182–83
early development of
A *1:* 22
eggs in
PS 2
festivals
A *1:* 196–97
goal of
A *1:* 186
gods of
A *1:* 190
impact of
PS 161
influence of
A *1:* 205–06
monastic system of
A *1:* 180
moral basis for
PS 122
as official religion
A *1:* 179–81
origin of
A *1:* 178–79
overview
A *1:* 177
rise of
A *1:* 8
spread of

A *1:* 182
suppression of
A *1:* 181–82
symbols of
A *1:* 191–93
texts of
A *1:* 189, 191
Western views of
A *1:* 189
worship practices of
A *1:* 193–95
See also Laozi; Religious
    Daoism; specific sects of
Daoist Canon
A *1:* 191
Daoist priest
PS 156 (ill.)
Daoist priests
A *1:* 193, 195 (ill.)
Daoist temple
PS 151 (ill.)
Daoist temples
A *1:* 195
Daoist thought, in everyday life
A *1:* 201
Daozang (Tao-tsang)
A *1:* 191
Darius I
A *2:* 450
B *2:* 405
Darius the Great
B *2:* 405
"Dark learning"
A *1:* 184
Darwin, Charles
A *1:* 15, 19, 33–34, 147
See also Huxley, Thomas
    Henry
"Darwin's bulldog"
A *1:* 29
Das Kapital (Marx)
B *2:* 263, 269
Dasam Granth
A *2:* 430–31
David (king)
A *2:* 346

Day for All Gods to Descend to
    Earth. *See* Chinese New Year
    festival
Day of rest, as pattern for working
    life
PS 6
Day of the Covenant holiday
A *1:* 82
Daya Ram
B *2:* 353–54
Dayananda Sarasvati
B *1:* **101–06,** 101 (ill.)
death
B *1:* 105
early life and travels
B *1:* 102–03
See also Arya Samaj sect
Dayananda Saraswati.
    See Dayananda Sarasvati
De (te) principle
A *1:* 162, 186–87
De Anima (Aristotle)
A *1:* 229
De Laplace, Pierre-Simon
A *1:* 26
De Lisieux, Thèrése
B *2:* 292
De Poetica (Aristotle)
A *1:* 229
Dead, realm of
PS 20
Dead Sea Scrolls
A *2:* 354–55
PS 11
Death, introduction of
PS 16
Death and rebirth. *See* Eleusinian
    mystery cults; Orphic mystery
    cults
Death rituals
    ancient Egypt
A *1:* 63
    Buddhist
A *1:* 113–14
    Christians
A *1:* 144–45

Confucian
A *1:* 171
Eastern Orthodox church
A *1:* 145
Mesopotamian
A *1:* 62
Neanderthals
A *1:* 5
December 25th, celebrations
A *1:* 15
Declaration of the Bab holiday
A *1:* 82
Deer Park
A *1:* 108
Deer Park Monastery
B *2:* 363
Degel (city)
B *2:* 377
Deities, classes of
A *1:* 5–6
Deities in Mahayana Buddhism
A *1:* 103
Deliverance from Error (Al-Ghazālī)
B *1:* 146
"Delusory" karma
A *2:* 332
Demeter
A *1:* 7, 222, 223
Demeter and Persephone
A *1:* 224
Democritus
A *1:* 24 (ill.), 215
Deng Xiaoping
A *1:* 182
Denmark, non-believers in
A *1:* 31
"Descent of Ishtar to the
    Underworld"
A *1:* 49
The Descent of Man (Darwin)
A *1:* 15, 33
Detachment, and Daoism
PS 150
Deuteronomy
B *2:* 283
See also Torah

Devi (goddess)
  A *2:* 242, 262
The Dhammapada
  A *1:* 100
  B *1:* 63, 65
  PS 165–74
  alterations to
  PS 173
  Canto III (The Mind)
  PS 169–70
  Canto XX (The Path)
  PS 170–72
  oral nature of
  PS 172–73
  texts of
  PS 168
Dharampala, Anagarika
  B *1:* **107–13**
  early life
  B *1:* 108
  mission visits
  B *1:* 110
  political activities
  B *1:* 112
  religious beliefs
  B *1:* 109–10
Dharamsala (India)
  B *1:* 95–96
Dharma
  A *2:* 248
  B *1:* 61, 115
  PS 111, 119, 169
  belief in
  A *1:* 99
Dharma Day
  A *1:* 108
Dharma wheel symbol
  A *2:* 335
Dharma wheel symbols
  A *1:* 101 (ill.)
Dharmachakra
  A *1:* 101 (ill.)
Dharmachakra mudra
  A *1:* 109
Dharmasastras
  A *2:* 265

D'Holbach, Baron
  A *1:* 32
Dhyana mudra
  A *1:* 109
"The Dialectic"
  B *2:* 258
Dialectic method
  A *1:* 216
"Dialectical materialism" concept
  B *2:* 264
Dialogues (Plato)
  A *1:* 232
Dialogues Concerning Natural Religion (Hume)
  A *1:* 26, 32
"Diamond Sutra"
  A *1:* 100
"Diamond Vehicle" Buddhism. *See* Vajrayana Buddhism
Diana (goddess)
  A *1:* 122
Diderot, Denis
  A *1:* 26
Dietary restrictions of, Bahá'í
  A *1:* 83
Dietary restrictions of Muslims
  A *2:* 315
Digambara sect
  A *2:* 328–29
  B *2:* 243
Din, Shams Ad-
  B *1:* 180, 181
Din al-Quanawi, Sadr Ad-
  B *1:* 181
Din Attar, Farid Od-
  B *1:* 180
Din Chelebi, Husan Ad-
  B *1:* 182
Din Muhaqqiq, Burhan Ad-
  B *1:* 180–81
Din Walad, Baha Ad-
  B *1:* 180
Din Zarkub, Salah Ad-
  B *1:* 182
Diocesan Congregation of the Calcutta Diocese. *See* Missionaries of Charity

Diogenes Laertius
  B *2:* 312
Dionysius
  A *1:* 222, 226
Dipa Ma
  B *1:* **115–20**, 116 (ill.)
  early life
  B *1:* 116
  teachings
  B *1:* 119
  travels
  B *1:* 120
Dipa Ma: The Life and Legacy of a Buddhist Master (Schmidt)
  B *1:* 120
Disciples of Jesus Christ
  A *1:* 121, 123
  See also individual apostles; individual disciples
"Disciplinary" vows
  A *2:* 341–42
Discrimination. *See* Apartheid
Divali festival
  A *2:* 339
"Diver" myth
  PS 4
Divination, by Druids
  A *2:* 381
Divine Comedy (Dante Alighieri)
  A *1:* 147, 235
Divine Liturgy
  A *1:* 140 (ill.)
Divinities, indigenous religions and
  A *2:* 273
Divorce
  Bahá'í views on
  A *1:* 83
  in Mesopotamia
  A *1:* 62
Diwali festival
  A *2:* 258–60, 341 (ill.)
Diwan-e Shams-e Tabriz-I (Rumi)
  B *1:* 182–83, 184
Djoser (pharaoh)
  A *1:* 52

Doctrine, arguments over in
Christianity
A *1:* 125–26
The Doctrine of the Mean
(Confucius)
A *1:* 163
B *1:* 88
PS 136
Dome of the Rock
A *2:* 294
Dominion of man over animals
PS 6
Dong Zhongshu
A *1:* 156–57
Door of Grace
PS 88
Door of Learning
PS 88
Door of Livelihood
PS 88
Door of Peace
PS 88
Doorkeeper of the Heart: Versions of Rābiʾa (Rābiʾa al-Adawiyah)
B *2:* 321–22
Doshas in Ayurveda
A *2:* 268
Dosojin festivals
A *2:* 407
Dove symbol
A *1:* 137–38
The Dream of the Red Chamber
A *1:* 174–75
Dreidel. *See* Hanukkah
(Chanukah) festival
Dress, traditional, in India
A *2:* 261
Druidic movements
A *2:* 381–82
Druidism
A *2:* 379–82
Druids
A *2:* 374
PS 97
Druids Friendly Society
A *2:* 382

Dualism
B *2:* 237
Duality, in religions
A *2:* 389
Duhka, explained
PS 166
Dukkha, concept of in Buddhism
A *1:* 96
Durga (universal mother)
A *2:* 260
Duzmin-Karaviev, Dimitri
B *2:* 360
Dvaita Vedanta
B *2:* 239

E

Ea (water god)
B *1:* 122
Ea/Enki (water god)
A *1:* 37, 61
Earth
PS creation of. *See specific creation stories*
Earth, date of creation
A *1:* 15
"Earth-bodied" beings
A *2:* 330
Easter
A *1:* 140
Eastern Orthodox Christianity
B *2:* 336, 360
Eastern Orthodox Church
after collapse of
Communism
A *1:* 130
establishment of
A *1:* 126–27, 132
Ottoman Turks and
A *1:* 128
weddings in
A *1:* 144
Ecclesiastes
PS 5
Ecclesiastical Ordinances (Calvin)

B *1:* 79
Ecology, Zoroastrianism and
PS 188
Edict of Worms
B *2:* 228–29, 230–31
Education
in Baháʾí faith
A *1:* 77–78, 83
importance of in
Confucianism
A *1:* 162–63
tradition of
A *1:* 147
Eggs, in creation accounts
PS 2
Egypt
ancient
A *1:* 43 (ill.)
architectural remains of
A *1:* 52
calendar of
A *1:* 66
conquering of
A *1:* 45
economic classes in
A *1:* 62
festivals in
A *1:* 42, 57–58, 63–64
gods of
A *1:* 61
medicine in
A *1:* 66
Mother Goddess in
A *1:* 7
religious rituals in
A *1:* 56–57, 57–59
role of priests in
A *1:* 52–53, 55
sciences and
A *1:* 66
tombs in
A *1:* 64 (ill.)
Egyptian Book of the Dead
A *1:* 42
Egyptian Muslims
A *2:* 299

Egyptian pharaoh
B *1:* 4–5
Egyptian religion, influence on
Judaism
A *1:* 8
Egyptian Sphinx
A *1:* 230
Egyptians
beliefs of
A *1:* 47–48
religions of
A *1:* 41–44
Eid ul Fitr
A *2:* 313
Eight Immortals (Ba Xian/Pa-hsien)
A *1:* 189, 192 (ill.), 193, 196
Eight Immortals Temple,
pilgrimages to
A *1:* 198
Eightfold Path
A *1:* 10–11, 90, 97–98
B *1:* 62
PS 166–67
Einstein, Albert
A *1:* 116; *2:* 367
Ekendriya beings
A *2:* 330
Ekhaka Sapa. *See* Black Elk
The Electronic Text Corpus of
Sumerian Literature **B** *1:* 125
Elder Troth
A *2:* 376
Eleatic School
A *1:* 214
"Election" concept
A *2:* 355
PS 10
Elektra (Sophocles)
A *1:* 211
Elenchus method
A *1:* 216
Eleusinian mystery cults
A *1:* 224
Eliot, T.S.
A *1:* 147
Elysium

A *2:* 223
Emanation theory
A *1:* 219; *2:* 220
Emerson, Ralph Waldo
A *1:* 93
Empedocles
A *1:* 215, 229
Emperor worship
A *1:* 222; *2:* 398
Emperor Wu
A *1:* 156
Empiricists
A *1:* 226
Encyclopedia of Religion (James)
A *1:* 21
Energy, categories of
A *2:* 268
Engaged Buddhism
B *2:* 360–61
Engels, Friedrich
B *2:* 260–261, 262 (ill.)
England, expulsion of
Jews from
A *2:* 348
Enheduanna
B *1:* **121–27,** 122 (ill.)
Enki (god of wisdom)
A *1:* 47
Enlightenment, Age of
A *1:* 25–26
Enlightenment concept
A *1:* 23, 129–30
Enlil (earth and storm god)
A *1:* 37, 42, 47, 61
B *1:* 122
Enuma Elish
A *1:* 41, 42, 48
Environment, respect for
A *2:* 460
Environmentalism, of Wiccans
PS 100
Eostre (goddess)
A *2:* 378
Ephriam (grandson of Jacob)
B *1:* 6
Epic and Classical Period of

Hinduism
A *2:* 241, 242
"The Epic of Creation"
A *1:* 41, 48–49
The Epic of Gilgamesh
A *1:* 7, 49
PS 61–72
Epictetus
A *1:* 218
Epicureanism
A *1:* 24, 218, 228
Episcopal Church
A *1:* 134
Episcopal Divinity School
(Massachusetts)
B *2:* 373
Equiria festival
A *1:* 233
Eqypt, organized religion in
A *1:* 37
Erh Ya
A *1:* 164
Eros, emergence of
PS 2
Eros, symbols of
A *1:* 230
Esau (son of Isaac)
B *1:* 6
Essay Concerning Human
Understanding (Locke)
B *2:* 268
The Essence of Christianity
(Feuerbach)
A *1:* 27, 32
The Essence of Judaism (Wise)
B *2:* 397
Essenes
A *2:* 350, 351, 355
Ethics
Greek philosophical views
about
A *1:* 227
and religion
A *1:* 16
Zoroastrianism and
A *2:* 452–53

Eucharist
   A *1:* 124, 138, 140 (ill.)
Eudemian Ethics (Aristotle)
   B *1:* 39–40
E-u-gim e-a (Hymn of Praise to Ekishnugal and Nanna on Assumption of En-ship)
   B *1:* 126
Euphrates River
   A *1:* 39
   B *1:* 3
Euridice
   A *1:* 225
Euripides
   A *1:* 211
Europe
   Mother Goddess in
   A *1:* 7
   Muslim countries and
   A *2:* 299–300
   non-believers in
   A *1:* 31
Euthydemus (Plato)
   B *2:* 316
Euthyphro (Plato)
   B *2:* 315
Evil spirits
   A *2:* 277–78
Evolution
   A *1:* 15, 29, 147
Evolution, and creation
   PS 4
"The Exaltation of Inana"
   A *1:* 54
   B *1:* 125
Exodus
   PS 11
   See also Torah
"Exodus" concept
   A *2:* 355
Exodus story
   B *2:* 282–83
Exorcism
   A *1:* 194
Expositions texts
   A *2:* 334

Extispicy, priests role in
   A *1:* 53
Extreme unction sacrament
   A *1:* 138–39, 144
Extremists
   A *2:* 321

F

Fadaʿih al-Batiniyya I (al-Ghazālī)
   B *1:* 148
Faerie Queen (Spenser)
   A *1:* 235
Faith, declaration of
   B *2:* 304
Faith-based theory of religion
   A *1:* 3–4
Families, Mesopotamian
   A *1:* 60
Family rituals
   A *1:* 166
Family shrines in Daoism
   A *1:* 194
Faqr
   B *1:* 13
Farabi, Abu al-Nasr Al-
   B *1:* 147
Faravahar (Farohar)
   PS 191
Faravahar symbol
   A *2:* 454–55, 454 (ill.)
Farel, Guillaume
   B *1:* 78
Farohar. *See* Faravahar symbol
Farvardigan festival
   A *2:* 459
Fasting
   A *1:* 141
   See also Ramadan
Father and mother, in creation myths
   PS 3
Father of All Spirits
   PS 3

Fatima (daughter of Muhammad)
   B *1:* 199
   as female ideal
   B *1:* 20
   Hand of
   B *1:* 18 (ill.)
   marriage of
   B *1:* 19
Fatima, pilgrimages to
   A *1:* 141
Fatimid dynasty
   A *2:* 299, 302
Fearlessness mudra
   A *1:* 109
Feast of the Valley festival
   A *1:* 58
Fellowship of Crotona
   B *1:* 139
Feminine principle, in Daoism
   PS 151
Feng Shui
   A *1:* 199
Festival of Fast Breaking
   A *2:* 313
Festival of Lights (Hanukkah)
   A *2:* 363 (ill.), 364
Festival of Osiris
   A *1:* 59
Festival of Ridvan
   A *1:* 72
   B *1:* 46
Festivals
   ancient Egypt
   A *1:* 42, 57–58, 63–64
   Daoist
   A *1:* 196–97
   Dosojin
   A *2:* 411
   Greek and Roman
   A *1:* 183, 231
   Hindu
   A *2:* 258–61
   Mesopotamian
   A *1:* 42, 60
   Shinto
   A *2:* 411–12

Sikhism
A *2:* 435–36
Spring
A *2:* 411
Fetterman, Lieutenant Colonel
William
B *1:* 53
Feuerbach, Ludwig
A *1:* 27, 31, 32
Fihi Ma Fih (Rumi)
B *1:* 183
Filial piety (xiao)
A *1:* 154
"Filioque" statement
A *1:* 131–32
Finch, Henry Clay
PS 195
Fire symbol, in Zoroastrianism
A *2:* 454
Fire temples
A *2:* 454
Fire urn
A *2:* 456
"Fire-bodied" beings
A *2:* 330
Fish symbol
A *1:* 137
Five Classics (Confucius)
A *1:* 156, 164
PS 136
Five Elements of Daoism
A *1:* 187–88, 188 (ill.)
Five emblems of Sikhism
A *2:* 431–32
Five Great Vows
A *2:* 327, 340
PS 121
"Five K's"
A *2:* 431–32
Five K's of Sikhism
B *1:* 158–59
Five Points of Calvinism
B *1:* 77
Five Precepts, recitation of
A *1:* 113
Five Relationships
A *1:* 161–62

Five seasons of Daoism
A *1:* 188
"Five Takhts"
A *2:* 437–38
"Five thieves"
A *2:* 429
Five Virtues of Confucianism
A *1:* 163
Five Vows of Jainism
B *2:* 246
"Five weapons"
A *2:* 429
Floating of the Water Lamps
ritual
A *1:* 196
Flower arranging
A *2:* 416
Flower of the Saints (Loyola)
B *2:* 218
Fodio, Muhammad
B *1:* 376
Fogmoon holiday
A *2:* 378
Folk religion
A *2:* 273
Folk Shinto
A *2:* 400
Folkish Asatru
A *2:* 376
Forced conversions of Sikhs
B *2:* 345
Forgiveness
A *1:* 121
Forn sed and Forn Sior
A *2:* 376
Foster, Mary E.
B *1:* 111
Foundation myths
PS 1–4
explained
PS 34
See also specific creation stories
"Four Affirmations"
A *2:* 403–04
"Four aims of Hinduism"
A *2:* 248

Four Books (Confucius)
PS 136
Four Books of Confucianism
A *1:* 163
Four elements of Empedocles
A *1:* 215
Four Noble Truths of Buddhism
A *1:* 97
B *1:* 70
PS 166–67
Four stages of life
A *2:* 248
Four Valleys (Bahá'u'lláh)
A *1:* 71
B *1:* 45
Four Vedas
A *2:* 251
Fox, George
A *1:* 134
Fragments/Cosmic Fragments
(Heraclitus)
A *1:* 229
Francis I, arrest of Protestants by
B *1:* 77
Fränkel, David
B *2:* 268
Frederick the Great
B *2:* 260–70
Freud, Sigmund
A *1:* 31, 32, 235
B *1:* 13
Frey (god)
A *2:* 378
Freya (Freyja) (goddess)
A *2:* 378
Frigg (Frigga)
A *2:* 378
Frog, symbol of fertility
A *1:* 230
Fuji, Mount
A *2:* 400, 412
Fulani people
B *2:* 376
PS 2
Fulani War
B *2:* 377–78

Funeral rites
   A *2:* 439–40, 461
Funeral traditions
   African
   A *2:* 277
   Chinese
   A *1:* 172
   Daoist
   A *1:* 200
   Greek
   A *1:* 235
The Future of an Illusion (Freud)
   A *1:* 32

G

Gabriel (angel)
   B *1:* 200
   See also Jabra'il (angel)
Gad (son of Jacob)
   B *1:* 6
Gaia (goddess)
   A *1:* 223
   PS 2, 3
Gaina Sutras
   PS 121, **137–47**
Gal Vihara Temple
   (Sri Lanka)
   A *1:* 114
Galilee
   A *1:* 121
Gamaliel
   B *2:* 302, 316
Games at Olympia
   A *1:* 233
Gandhi, Indira
   A *2:* 425
Gandhi, Mahatma
   B *1:* **129–36,** 129 (ill.)
   children dressed as
   B *1:* 132 (ill.)
   early life
   B *1:* 129–36
   education
   B *1:* 130

racism experienced by
   B *1:* 130–32
in South Africa
   B *1:* 131–33
Gandhi, Mohandas K.
   A *2:* 264, 266, 342
Ganesh (god)
   A *2:* 262
Ganga River (Ganges River)
   A *2:* 256
Garden of Ridvan
   A *1:* 72
Gardner, Gerald Brousseau
   B *1:* **137–44,**
     137 (ill.)
   PS 101
   early life
   B *1:* 138
   religious explorations
   B *1:* 139
Gardner, Grissell
   B *1:* 138
The Gathas
   A *2:* 453
   B *2:* 400
   PS 185–89
   about
   PS 122
   composition and
     arrangement of
   PS 185–86
   history of
   PS 187–88
Gathic Avestan
   A *2:* 453
   PS 188
Gaudiya Vaishnavism
   B *1:* 67–68, 69, 72–73
Gaura. *See* Caitanya Mahaprabhu
Gautama, Maha-Pajapati
   B *1:* 71, 72
Geb (god)
   A *1:* 43
Gelug. *See* Tibetan Buddhism
Geluk. *See* Tibetan Buddhism
Gemara (commentaries)

   A *2:* 356
Genesis, chapters of
   PS 7–10
   creation story principles in
   PS 6
   themes of
   PS 10–11
   See also Babylonian Genesis;
     Tanakh; Torah
Genesis, questioning of
   A *1:* 28
Geneva, under Calvinism
   B *1:* 80
Genghis Khan
   A *1:* 185
Genmei (empress)
   A *2:* 405
   PS 15
Geocentrism concept
   A *1:* 236
Geography
   A *1:* 46; *2:* 273
Geology, Christian creation
   concepts and
   A *1:* 28
German heathenism
   A *2:* 376
German Ideology (Marx)
   B *2:* 260
German Jewish Enlightenment
   B *2:* 272–73
Gershwin, George
   A *2:* 369
Gershwin, Ira
   A *2:* 369
Ghazālī, Abu Hāmid
   Muhammad al-
   B *1:* **145–51**
   career
   B *1:* 147–48
   early life
   B *1:* 145–46
   education
   B *1:* 146–47
   Sufism and
   B *1:* 148–49

Ghost Dance
  B *1:* 54–55
Gilgamesh. *See The Epic of Gilgamesh*
Girnar, Mount
  A *2:* 339
Glaysher, Frederick
  A *1:* 77
Global community, belief of in Bahá'í faith
  A *1:* 78–79
The Glorious Mysteries
  A *2:* 257
Gobind Rai Sodhi. *See* Gobind Singh (Guru)
Gobind Singh (Guru)
  A *2:* 423
  B *1:* **153–61**, 154 (ill.)
Gobind Singh Ji, Guru
  PS 86
God
  aspects of in Christianity
    A *1:* 126
  aspects of in Judaism
    A *2:* 352–54
  aspects of in Sikhism
    A *2:* 427–28
  concept of in Sikhism
    PS 85–86
  goodness created by
    PS 6
  Islamic belief in
    A *2:* 303–04
  love of
    A *1:* 121
  names of
    A *1:* 9–10, 42; *2:* 276
    PS 23, 36
  nature of
    A *1:* 214
    PS 36, 109–10, 176
  need for
    A *1:* 31
  oneness of
    PS 175–76
  personal experience of

  A *1:* 133–34
  purpose for
    A *1:* 32
  writing conventions for name of
    PS 7
God, many names of
  B *2:* 238
God Passes By (Shoghi Effendi)
  A *1:* 74
  PS 178
God's prophets, oneness of
  PS 176
A Goddess Arrives (Gardner)
  B *1:* 139
Goddess Spirituality movements
  PS 97
Goddess worship
  A *2:* 382–84
Godparents, role of in Daoism
  A *1:* 200
Gods
  as aspects of nature
    A *1:* 16
  classes of in Asatru
    A *2:* 377
  depicted as animals
    A *1:* 42
  Egyptian
    A *1:* 37, 61
Gods and goddesses
  A *1:* 55–56; *2:* 246 (ill.)
Gods and goddesses of Mesopotamia
  B *1:* 122
Gods of Sumer
  A *1:* 41
Golden Rule
  PS 126
Golden Temple. *See* Amritsar (city)
Goldman, Emma
  PS 196 (ill.)
  about
    PS 193 95
  beliefs of
    PS 201

Goldstein, Joseph
  B *1:* 120
Gomatesvara statue
  A *2:* 339
Gomorrah
  B *1:* 5, 6
Gonxha Bojaxhiu, Agnes. *See* Mother Teresa
Good and evil, Daoist view of
  PS 152
Good Friday
  A *1:* 141
Good government. *See* Confucianism
Good living, fourteen rules for
  B *2:* 363–64
Goodness, as creation of God
  PS 6
Gorgias (Plato)
  B *2:* 315
Gospel According to Saint Matthew
  Chapter 5
    PS 207–09
  Chapter 6
    PS 209–10
  Chapter 7
    PS 210–11
Gospel of John
  A *1:* 137
Gospel of Luke
  A *1:* 137
Gospel of Mark
  A *1:* 137
Gospel of Matthew
  A *1:* 137
Grant, Ulysses S.
  B *2:* 396
Granth, Sri Guru
  A *2:* 423, 429–30, 429 (ill.)
  B *1:* 161–62
  PS 86–87, 87 (ill.)
Granthi
  PS 87
Gravitation, law of
  A *1:* 26

Great Dao
    A *1:* 185–86
    See also Daoism
"Great Epic of the Bharata
    Dynasty"
    A *2:* 253
The Great Learning (Confucius)
    A *1:* 163
    B *1:* 88
    PS 136
Great Mother, worship of
    A *1:* 7
"Great Pharmacopaeia"
    A *1:* 202
Great Pure
    A *1:* 188
Great Revolt
    A *2:* 346, 348
"Great Urn Festival"
    A *2:* 260
Great Vows of Mahavira
    PS 137–38, 145
Greatest Name symbol
    A *1:* 80
**Greco-Roman Religion and
    Philosophy**
    A *1:* 207–38
    about
    A *1:* 212, 214
    impact of
    A *1:* 235–36
    main beliefs of
    A *1:* 226
    overview
    A *1:* 207–08, 210
    See also specific philosophers
Greek
    A *1:* 220–22
    hierarchy of
    A *1:* 6
    Mesopotamian
    A *1:* 37, 53, 61
    Roman view of
    A *1:* 220
Greek mythology, eggs in
    PS 2

Greek religion
    beginnings of
    A *1:* 210, 212–13
    festivals
    A *1:* 183, 231, 233
    gods and goddesses of
    A *1:* 207, 225 (ill.)
    growth of
    A *1:* 210–11
    See also specific gods and
        goddesses
Green, Graham
    A *1:* 147
Green Mountain Dharma Center
    and Maple Forest Monastery
    B *2:* 363
Grihasthya stage
    A *2:* 248
Group Areas Act
    B *2:* 371, 372 (ill.)
Group behavior
    B *1:* 166–67
Guardian, role of in Bahá'í faith
    A *1:* 76
"Guide for the Perplexed"
    (Maimonides)
    A *2:* 354
    B *2:* 256
Gurdwaras
    A *2:* 432–34
    B *2:* 357
    PS 87, 88
Guru
    B *2:* 235
Gurupurabs (Gurupurbs) holiday
    A *2:* 436
Gurus, of Sikhism
    A *2:* 421–23

Ⓗ

Hades
    A *1:* 222, 223, 224
Hadith
    PS 30
Hadith, development of

B *1:* 28
Hadiths
    A *2:* 309–10
    B *2:* 300
Hafsa (wife of Muhammad)
    B *2:* 304
Haft-Vádí ("Seven Valleys")
    PS 177
Hagar
    B *1:* 5, 6
"Hail to the Jewel in the Lotus"
    A *1:* 104
Haiti, Vodou in
    A *2:* 280
Haj (pilgrimage to Mecca)
    A *2:* 306, 314–15
    B *1:* 200 (ill.); *2:* 286 (ill.)
Halal, defined
    PS 24
Hall of Maat
    A *1:* 48
Halloween
    A *2:* 390
Hallucinogenic substances, use of
    A *2:* 274
Ham (son of Noah)
    B *1:* 3
Hamaspathmaidyem festival
    A *2:* 458
Hammurabi
    A *1:* 41
Hammurabi, Mesopotamian law of
    PS 205
Han Dynasty
    A *1:* 156
    development of Daoism
    A *1:* 179
    PS 135
Han Xianzi (god)
    A *1:* 190, 193
Hana Matsuri
    A *1:* 108
Hanafi legal tradition
    PS 30
Hanbali legal tradition
    PS 30

Hands of the Cause of God
    A *1:* 75, 76
Ha-ne-go-ate-geh (Evil Minded)
    A *2:* 286
Hanukkah (Chanukah) festival
    A *1:* 15; *2:* 346, 363–64,
        363 (ill.)
Hanuman (god)
    A *2:* 262
Happiness. *See* Aristotle
Har Gobind (Guru)
    B *1:* 155
Har Rai, Guru
    A *2:* 423
Haram, defined
    PS 24
Haran (brother of Abraham)
    B *1:* 2
Haran (city)
    B *1:* 3
Hare Krishna movement
    B *1:* 72–73
    See also Caitanya Mahaprabhu;
        Chaitanyas
Hargobind, Guru
    A *2:* 422, 437
Haridwar (city)
    A *2:* 260
Harkrishan, Guru
    A *2:* 423
Harmony
    B *2:* 205 (ill.)
Harmony, emphasis on in Shinto
    A *2:* 414–15
Harrer, Heinrich
    B *1:* 94
Haruspices
    A *1:* 231
Hasan (son of Fatima)
    B *1:* 19
Hasidic ceremonies
    B *1:* 175 (ill.)
Hasidism (Chasidism)
    A *2:* 351
    B *1:* 174–77; *2:* 271
Hauravatat

A *2:* 451
Hauravatat concept
    PS 186
Hausaland (Africa)
    B *1:* 102
Hawan
    A *2:* 456
Ha-wen-ne-yu
    (Great Spirit)
    A *2:* 286
Haymarket Square bombing
    PS 194–95
He Xiangu (god)
    A *1:* 190
Head coverings, in Sikhism
    A *2:* 433
Head shaving
    B *1:* 72
"Heart Sutra"
    A *1:* 100
Heaven
    A *1:* 135–36
    See also nirvana concept
        Heaven, Muhammad's
        visit to
    B *2:* 303
Heavenly Pillar
    PS 17
Hebrew Bible
    PS 203
    See also Tanakh
Hebrew Union College
    B *2:* 391, 394, 395
Hedensk sed
    A *2:* 376
Hegel, Georg Wilhelm Friedrich
    B *2:* 264
Hekhaka Sapa. *See* Black Elk
Heliopolis
    A *1:* 43
Hellenistic philosophy
    A *1:* 217
Heng Shan Bei mountain
    A *1:* 198
Heng Shan Nan mountain
    A *1:* 198

He-no (god)
    A *2:* 286
Henotheistic religions
    A *2:* 246
Hephaestus
    A *1:* 222
Hera
    A *1:* 221, 223
Heraclitus
    A *1:* 213, 221, 227, 229
    B *1:* 27
Herbalists, in indigenous religions
    A *2:* 278
Hermes
    A *1:* 66, 222
Hermias of Atarneus
    B *1:* 35, 43
Hermits of Saint Augustine
    B *2:* 226
Herne
    A *2:* 380
"Heroic Age of the Bahá'í Faith"
    A *1:* 69
Hesiod
    A *1:* 210–11, 228
Hess, Moses
    B *2:* 265
Hess, Rudolf
    A *2:* 377
Hestia
    A *1:* 222–23
Hewavitarne, (Don) David.
    See Anagarika Dharmapala
Hewavitarne, Mallika
    B *1:* 108
The Hidden Words of Bahá'u'lláh
    A *1:* 71; *2:* 404
    B *1:* 45
    PS 14–15, **175–84**
    similarities to other religious
        works
    PS 183
    structure of
    PS 178–79
    See also Bahá'í Hijrah of
        Muhammad Hieda no Are

High Magic's Aid (Gardner)
  B *1:* 140
Himmat Rai
  B *2:* 354
Himmler, Heinrick
  A *2:* 377
Hinayana Buddhism.
  See Theravada Buddhism
Hindu terms of respect
  B *2:* 235
Hindu thought
  PS 111, 119
Hinduism
  A *2:* **239–69**
  about
  A *2:* 243
  basic theological principles of
  A *2:* 249
  defined
  A *2:* 240
  deities of
  A *2:* 262
  disciplines of
  A *2:* 249–50
  festivals
  A *2:* 258–61
  followers of
  PS 119
  major divisions of
  A *2:* 241
  monotheism of
  A *1:* 9
  origins of
  A *2:* 241
  overview
  A *2:* 239
  places of worship in
  A *2:* 258
  spread of
  A *2:* 266
  supreme being in creation stories
  PS 3
  supreme god of
  A *2:* 246
  PS 119
  three classes of

A *2:* 244
worship in
  A *2:* 256–58
  See also "Paper on Hinduism"
Hippias Minor and Major (Plato)
  B *2:* 315
Hira, Mount
  A *2:* 292
  B *1:* 195 (ill.)
Hiroshima
  A *2:* 416
Hispaniola, Vodou in
  A *2:* 280
*The History of the Isrealite Nation
  from Abraham to the Present
  Time* (Wise)
  B *2:* 397
Hokekyo. *See* Lotus Sutra
Hola Mohalla festival
  A *2:* 426, 436
Holbach, Paul Henri de
  A *1:* 26
Holocaust
  A *2:* 349
Holy Communion
  A *1:* 138, 143
Holy day of Mahavira Jayanti
  A *2:* 339
Holy days, in Bahá'í faith
  A *1:* 80–82
Holy Land
  pilgrimages to
  A *1:* 141
  See also Jerusalem
Holy of Holies
  A *2:* 346
Holy orders
  A *1:* 138
Holy Spirit
  B *2:* 308–09
"Holy Spirit." *See* Zoroastrianism
Home worship, in Buddhism
  A *1:* 105–06
Homer
  A *1:* 210, 228
Homeric Hymns

A *1:* 228
Ho-no-che-no-keh
  (Invisible Agents)
  A *2:* 286
Honor killings
  B *1:* 199
Ho-nun-den-ont
  (Keepers of the Faith)
  A *2:* 287
Hoover, J. Edgar
  PS 201
Hopi Indians, creation/
  foundation myths of
  PS 3
Horus (god)
  A *1:* 44, 46 (ill.)
  described
  A *1:* 61
  war with Set
  A *1:* 41, 48
Householders, religious duties of
  A *2:* 340
Houses of Worship
  (Mashriqu'l-Adhkar)
  A *1:* 80–81
Hsun Tzu. *See* Confucianism
Hua Shan mountain
  A *1:* 198
Huainanzi (Huai-nan-tzu)
  A *1:* 191
Huangdi (Yellow Emperor)
  A *1:* 179
Huanglao masters
  A *1:* 179
Huddleston, Father Trevor
  B *2:* 368–69
Human activity, gods
  responsibility for areas of
  A *1:* 46
Humanism, Marx's views on
  B *2:* 264
Humanism, rise of
  A *1:* 129
Humanistic Judaism, creator-god
  concept in
  A *1:* 19–20

Humanity, oneness of
  PS 176
Humankind, as greatest creation
  of God
  PS 6
Humans, five ages of
  A *1:* 228
Humans, uniqueness of
  PS 6
Hume, David
  A *1:* 26, 32
Humility, in Daoism
  A *1:* 187
Hundred Schools of Thought
  B *1:* 84
Hursag
  A *1:* 40
Husayn (son of Fatima)
  B *1:* 19
Hutosa (queen of Bactria)
  A *2:* 447
  B *2:* 403
Huxley, Thomas Henry
  A *1:* 28, 29
  PS 4
Hyksos invasion
  A *1:* 44
Hymn of Praise to Enheduanna
  B *1:* 126
"Hymn to Ra"
  A *1:* 54
Hymns of Zarathushtra.
  See The Gathas

I

I and the Village (Chagall)
  A *2:* 369
Iberia, Muslim occupation of
  A *2:* 295
Ibn Affan, Uthman/Usman
  PS 29
Ibn al-Arabi
  B *2:* 343
Ibn Isma'il Bukhari, Muhammad
  A *2:* 309–10

Ibn Khaldun
  B *1:* **163–69,** 164 (ill.)
  at Qalat ibn Salama
  B *1:* 166–67
Ibrahim. *See* Abraham
Idols
  destruction of
  B *1:* 2
  worship of
  B *1:* 156, 195–96
  See also Ka'aba
Iftar meal
  A *2:* 313
Ihya' 'Ulum ad-Din
  (al-Ghazālī)
  B *1:* 149
Ikhnaton. *See* Akhenaten
Iliad (Homer)
  A *1:* 210, 228
Imam Ali. *See* 'Ali Abī ibn Tālib
Imam title
  A *2:* 302
Imams
  B *1:* 43
Imbolc
  A *2:* 381, 388
Immaculate Conception
  B *1:* 190
Immortality
  hero's search for
  A *1:* 7
  Plato's views on
  A *1:* 227–28
  transmigration of souls and
  A *1:* 227
"Imperial Rescript on Education"
  act
  A *2:* 398
Imperial Way Buddhism
  B *2:* 313
Implicit atheism
  A *1:* 30
Imported religions, assimilation
  of
  A *2:* 273
Inan, Abu

B *1:* 165
Inanna (fertility/war goddess)
  B *1:* 122, 124, 125 (ill.)
Inanna (goddess)
  A *1:* 37–38, 40, 53
  See also Ishtar (goddess)
Inanna Ziggurat
  A *1:* 57
Incarnation
  A *1:* 135
The Incoherence of the Philosophers
  (al-Ghazālī)
  B *1:* 147
India
  early Hinduism in
  A *1:* 8
  Mother Goddess in
  A *1:* 7
  Protestantism in
  A *1:* 96
  secularism of
  A *2:* 268–69
India (British), division of
  A *2:* 425
India, language of
  PS 173
Indian National Congress party
  B *1:* 134
Indigenous Religions
  A *2:* **271–90**
  about
  A *2:* 276
  effect of Christianity and
    Islam on
  A *2:* 278–79
  overview
  A *2:* 271–73
  practicers of
  A *2:* 272–73
  ritual activities of
  A *2:* 273
  shamans/diviners in
  A *2:* 274–75
  types of
  A *2:* 271
  written texts and

A *2:* 273

See also African indigenous
    religions
Individual action
    PS 196
Indrabetta hill
    A *2:* 339
Indulgences
    A *1:* 129
    B *2:* 227
Indus Valley culture,
    and Hinduism
    A *2:* 241
"Inerrancy," of the Bible
    A *1:* 34
*In-nin-sa-gur-ra (Stouthearted
    Lady)* (Enheduanna)
    B *1:* 126
Innumerable Meaning Sutra
    B *2:* 299
Inquisition
    A *1:* 128
*Inscription on Visualizing Spirits
    and Refining Vital Breath*
    (Sun Sumiao)
    A *1:* 202
Insight Meditation Society
    B *1:* 120
Institutes of the Christian Religion
    (Calvin)
    B *1:* 77, 80
"Intelligent design"
    A *1:* 15–16, 28
International Bahá'í Council
    A *1:* 76
International Community
    A *1:* 84
International Confucian Festival
    A *1:* 167
International Society for Krisna
    Consciousness
    A *2:* 242, 244
"The Intimate Biography
    of Han Emperor Wu"
    (Mao Shan)
    A *1:* 205

Ion (Plato)
    B *2:* 315
Ionian School
    B *1:* 26
Iran, Islamic Revolution in
    A *2:* 300
Iraq, Mother Goddess
    worship in
    A *1:* 6
Iroguois tribe
    A *2:* 286–87
Isaac (son of Abraham)
    B *1:* 5, 6–7
Isaiah. *See* Nevi'im
Ishmael
    B *1:* 5, 6
Ishtar (goddess)
    described
    A *1:* 61
    journey to underword by
    A *1:* 48–49
    ritual marriage of
    A *1:* 53
    See also Inanna
        (fertility/war goddess)
Ishtar Ziggurat
    A *1:* 57
Ishvar Puri
    B *1:* 69
Isis (goddess)
    A *1:* 43, 46 (ill.), 61
Islam
    A *2:* **291–321**
    about
    A *2:* 295
    battles
    B *1:* 21 (ill.), 30
    beliefs of
    A *2:* 303–06
    and Christianity
    A *1:* 127; *2:* 3–5
    converts to
    B *2:* 288
    daily life of
    A *2:* 315–16
    divisions within

A *2:* 297–98
    extremists within
    A *2:* 300–01
    five pillars of
    B *1:* 1
    influence of
    A *2:* 316–21
    leadership of
    A *2:* 302
    overview
    A *2:* 291–92
    rise of
    A *1:* 8, 127
    role of Ishmael in
    B *1:* 8
    schisms in
    B *1:* 19–23
    sectarian conflict within
    B *2:* 292
    sects of
    A *2:* 301–03
    similarity of Zoroastrianism to
    PS 191–92
    spread of
    A *2:* 296–97, 297 (ill.), 300
    status of women in
    B *1:* 199
    supreme being in creation
        accounts of
    PS 3
    symbolic behavior of
    A *1:* 310
    tolerance for other faiths
    B *2:* 290
    See also hadiths; Muhammad;
        Muslims; Shi'ite Muslims;
        Sufism; Sunni Muslims
Islamic constitution
    B *2:* 290
Islamic empire,
    capitals of
    A *2:* 298
Islamic law
    A *2:* 300
Islamic prayer unit
    A *2:* 312–13

Islamic Revolution (Iran)
A *2:* 300
Isma'ili, Abu Nasr Al-
B *1:* 146
Ismailis
A *2:* 299
Israel
creation of
A *2:* 349–50
sacred sites in
A *2:* 364–65
Israel, twelve tribes of
B *1:* 6, 7
Israelites
B *2:* 279, 282
Israfil (angel)
A *2:* 309
PS 24
Issac (son of Abraham)
B *1:* 6, 7
Issachar (son of Jacob)
B *1:* 6
Isthmian Games
A *1:* 233
Ithman
A *2:* 298
Ivory Coast
B *2:* 343–44
Iwa, in Vodou religions
A *2:* 281, 282
Iyengar, B. K. S.
A *2:* 267
Izanagi
PS 18 (ill.)
children of
PS 3
in Shinto creation story
PS 14, 15
shrines to
PS 21
Izanami
PS 18 (ill.)
children of
PS 3
in Shinto creation story
PS 14

shrines to
PS 21

J

Jabra'il (angel)
A *2:* 292–93, 309
B *1:* 200; *2:* 287–88, 289
PS 23–24
Jacob (son of Isaac)
B *1:* 6, 7
Jade Emperor
A *1:* 196
Jade Emperor Assembly
A *1:* 196
Jade Pure
A *1:* 188
Ja'fari legal tradition
PS 30
Jahangir (emperor)
A *2:* 423
B *2:* 351
Jain cosmic wheel
B *2:* 245 (ill.)
Jain Dharma. *See* Jainism
"Jain menu"
A *2:* 342
Jain scriptures
A *2:* 333–34
Jainism
A *2:* **323–43,** 331 (ill.)
about
A *2:* 326
concept of creator-god and
A *1:* 23; *2:* 323, 329
cycles of time
B *2:* 244–45
divisions of
B *2:* 243
holidays of
A *2:* 339
influences of
A *2:* 342–43
monotheism and
A *1:* 8

moral basis for
PS 121
origins of
A *2:* 325
overview
A *2:* 323
philosophy of life of
PS 145
pilgrimages of
A *2:* 339–40
prayers of
A *2:* 335–36
sacred texts of
PS 137–38
sects of
A *2:* 328
similarity to Buddhism and
Hinduism
PS 146
spread of
A *2:* 327–28
sutras recited by
A *2:* 336
vegetarianism and
A *2:* 342
PS 140
See also jiva
Jains, number of
A *2:* 323, 325
PS 146
See also specific sects of
Jalāl ad-Dīn ar-Rūmī
B *1:* **179–85,** 179 (ill.);
2: 343–44
early life
B *1:* 180
poetry
B *1:* 181–82, 184–85
travels
B *1:* 180
James, George Alfred
A *1:* 21
James (Saint)
B *2:* 305
James II
B *2:* 231

Jamshed-e Navroz holiday
A *2:* 458
Janam Sakhis
A *2:* 431
Janus (god)
A *1:* 231
Japan
PS 3, 15
Buddhism in
A *1:* 92; *2:* 395
Confucianism in
A *1:* 158
non-believers in
A *1:* 31
religious tradition in
A *1:* 95
surrender of
A *2:* 398
symbols of
A *2:* 407–08
Japan, Mongol invasion of
B *2:* 295, 309
Japanese/American relations
A *2:* 396–97
Japanese civilization, origins of
A *2:* 395
Japanese Confucianism
A *1:* 172–73
Jashan-e Mehragan festival
A *2:* 459
Jashan-e Sedah festival
A *2:* 459
Jashan-e Tirigan festival
A *2:* 459
Jehovah's Witnesses
A *1:* 130
Jeremiah. *See* Nevi'im
Jerusalem
conquering of
A *2:* 294
first Temple in
A *2:* 346
pilgrimage to
A *1:* 141
reclaiming of
A *2:* 299
second Temple in

A *2:* 346
See also Crusades
Jerusalem; or, On Religious
Power and Judaism
(Mendelssohn)
B *2:* 279
Jerusalem Talmud. *See* Talmud
Jesuit missionaries, in China
A *1:* 159
Jesuits. *See* Society of Jesus
(Jesuit order)
Jesus Christ
B *1:* **187–93,** 187 (ill.),
192 (ill.)
about
PS 205
adulthood
B *1:* 190–92
birth and baptism of
A *1:* 15, 131 (ill.)
childhood of
A *1:* 121
crucifixion and death of
A *1:* 122–23, 123
death
B *1:* 192
early life
B *1:* 188–89
message of
PS 204
as a prophet
PS 24
restorative powers of
A *1:* 121
resurrection of
A *1:* 123, 131 (ill.)
teachings of
A *1:* 121
See also Christianity;
New Testament; Sermon
on the Mount
Jesus Christ, Second Coming of
A *1:* 130
Jesus of Nazareth. *See* Jesus Christ
Jetsun Jamphel Ngawang Lobsang
Yeshe Tenzin Gyatso.
See Dalai Lama

Jewish holidays
A *2:* 361
See also Hanukkah
(Chanukah) festival;
Passover; Rosh Hashanah;
Yom Kippur
Jewish prayer service,
components of
A *2:* 360–61
Jewish rights movement.
See Mendelssohn
Jewish Theological Seminary
B *2:* 395
Jewish tradition. *See Commentary
on the Mishnah* (Maimonides)
Jews
birth of
B *1:* 6
discrimination against
B *2:* 392
isolation of
B *2:* 272
treatment of in World War II
B *2:* 339–40
The Jews (Lessing)
B *2:* 269
Jews, enslavement of
A *2:* 346
Jiao ritual
A *1:* 193–94
Jihad. *See* Usuman Dan Fodio
Jina (conqueror)
A *2:* 325, 329
PS 139
Jinas, nature of
B *2:* 243
Jinn spirits
A *2:* 305
Jiva (soul)
PS 138
Jiva (soul), six forms of
A *2:* 330–31
Jochebed, mother of Moses
B *2:* 285
Jomon period
A *2:* 395

Jonas, Regina
B *2:* 214
Jordan River
B *1:* 3
Jotnar class
A *2:* 377
The Joyful Mysteries
A *2:* 257
Judah (son of Jacob)
B *1:* 6
Judah Maccabee
A *2:* 364
Judaism
A *2:* **345–70,** 359 (ill.)
about
A *2:* 349
core beliefs of
A *2:* 352–54
cultural aspects of
A *2:* 365–66
denominations of
B *2:* 394
divisions within
A *2:* 350–51, 351–52
influence of Zoroastrainism on
A *2:* 452
in medieval Spain
B *2:* 250
monotheism and
A *1:* 25; *2:* 346
overview
A *2:* 345
rise of
A *1:* 8
role of Abraham in
B *1:* 1
supreme being in creation
accounts of
PS 3
symbols of
A *2:* 356–59
Zoroastrianism and
PS 188, 191–92
See also Tanakh
Judaism and Christianity,
Their Agreements and

Disagreements (Wise)
B *2:* 397
Judaism, Its Doctrines and
Duties (Wise)
B *2:* 397
Judas Iscariot
A *1:* 122
B *1:* 192
Judgment of the Dead trial
A *1:* 48
Judith in the Tent of Holofernes
(Johann Liss)
A *2:* 268
Juno
A *1:* 122
Junzi (chun-tze) principle
A *1:* 161
"Jup"
about
PS 85–86
See also Sri Guru Granth Sahib
Jupiter
A *1:* 122, 230
"Justification by faith alone" belief
A *1:* 133
Juwayni, Abu al-Malik Al-
B *1:* 147

K

Ka soul
A *1:* 47, 55
Ka'aba
building of
B *1:* 8
casting idols from
B *2:* 305
ownership of
B *1:* 26, 196
pilgrimages to
B *2:* 287
Ka'aba shrine
A *2:* 292, 314–15, 314 (ill)
Kaang (god)
PS 3
Kabbalah

B *1:* 173
Kabir
A *2:* 265
Kaccha
B *1:* 159
Kaddish prayer
A *2:* 360–61
Kagutsuchi (god)
PS 14
Kaimoku Sho (Nichiren)
B *2:* 296
Kalam philosophy
B *1:* 147
Kali (goddess)
A *2:* 259, 262
Kalighat Home for the Dying
B *2:* 293
Kalimat-i-Maknunih
(The Hidden Words)
A *1:* 71
PS 122–23, 175
Kama
A *2:* 248
Kamayut Meditation Center
B *1:* 117
Kami
A *2:* 395, 402, 403, 410
Kami spirits
PS 14, 15
Kamikaze pilots
A *2:* 398
Kamya rituals
A *2:* 258
Kanga
B *1:* 159
Kant, Immanuel
A *1:* 26
B *2:* 275
Kanzo ritual
A *2:* 281
Kapha (lubrication/structure
energy)
A *2:* 268
Kara
A *2:* 432
B *1:* 159

Karbala, battle at
  A *2:* 298
Karma
  B *2:* 252–53
  PS 88, 119, 138
  Jain concept of
  A *2:* 332
  nature of
  A *2:* 332
  types of
  A *2:* 263, 332
  See also Reincarnation
Karma yoga
  A *2:* 250
Kasha (kachh)
  A *2:* 431
Kashrut
  A *2:* 365
Katha function
  A *2:* 433
Kathina, festival of
  A *1:* 108
Kaur, taking name of
  B *2:* 354
Kesh
  A *2:* 431
  B *1:* 158
Keshadharis sect
  A *2:* 426
Keturah (wife of Abraham)
  B *1:* 7
Ketuvin (Writings)
  A *2:* 354
  PS 5
Khadijah
  B *1:* **195–202;** *2:* 301
  business activities
  B *1:* 196–97, 198
  early life
  B *1:* 195–96
  family life
  B *1:* 199–200
  self-exile
  B *1:* 201
Khalsa
  A *2:* 427

Khalsa creation
  B *2:* 353–54
Khanda symbol
  A *2:* 431 (ill.), 432
Khanum, Khadijih
  B *1:* 41
Kharijites
  B *1:* 30
Khashathra Vairya
  A *2:* 451
Khashathra Vairya concept
  PS 186
Khawf
  B *1:* 13
Kheiralla, Ibrahim George
  A *1:* 74
Khordad Sal
  A *2:* 459
Khorsabad, winged bull
    sculptures at
  A *1:* 51
Khorshed Niyaesh prayer
  A *2:* 456
Khuddakanikaya
  PS 168
King Jr., Martin Luther
  A *2:* 264
  B *2:* 360–61
Kirpan
  A *2:* 432
  B *2:* 159
Kirtan function
  A *2:* 433
Kitab al-ʿibar (Universal History)
    (Ibn Khaldūn)
  B *1:* 163, 166, 167–68
Kitab-i-Aqdas (Book of Laws)
  A *1:* 79
  B *1:* 41, 55–56
  PS 177
Kitab-i-Iqan
    (The Book of Certitude)
  A *1:* 71, 79
  B *1:* 45
  PS 177

Kitchen God, ascension of
  A *1:* 197
Kiya (wife of Akhenaten)
  B *1:* 13–14
Kiyosumidera monastery
  B *2:* 294
Klerk, F. W. De
  B *2:* 373
Knossos
  A *1:* 6
Knowledge
  A *1:* 226–27
"Knowledge of the Weapon"
    sutra
  PS 137, 141–45
"Knowledge-obscuring"
    karma
  A *2:* 332
Knox, John
  A *1:* 133
Koans
  A *1:* 96
Kodashim (Holy Things)
  A *2:* 356
Kojiki
  nature of
  PS 14–15
  parts of
  PS 13–14
Kojiki text
  A *2:* 395–96, 404–06
Kong (Kʾung). *See* Confucius
Kong Chiu. *See* Confucianism
Kong Fuzi (Kʾung Fu-tzu).
    See Confucius
Kong Qiu. *See* Confucianism
Kongo tribes
  A *2:* 281
Kongzi (Kʾung-tzu).
    See Confucius
Koran. *See* Qurʾan
Korea
  Confucianism in
  A *1:* 158
  religious tradition in
  A *1:* 95

spread of Buddhism in
A *1:* 92
Korean Confucianism
A *1:* 172
Kornfield, Jack
B *1:* 120
Kosher dietary laws
A *2:* 365
Kris and Other Malay Weapons
(Gardner)
B *1:* 138
Krishna (god)
A *2:* 241, 262
B *2:* 236 (ill.)
PS 119
See also Gaudiya Vaishna-
vism; Mahabharata
Kriyamani Karma
A *2:* 263
Ksatriyas (caste)
A *2:* 263
B *2:* 248
Kshnoon movement
A *2:* 449
Kuan Yin
A *1:* 95, 103
Kubra, Khadijah Al-.
See Khadijah
Kukas group
A *2:* 426
Kumbh Mela (Urn Festival)
A *2:* 260–61, 264 (ill.)
Kung Family Mansion
A *1:* 169
K'ung Fu-tzu.
See Confucius
Kungha
A *2:* 431
Kuresh
B *2:* 330
Kushti (koshti) symbol
A *2:* 454, 456
Kusinagar, pilgrimages to
A *1:* 108
Kusti (Holy Path)
A *2:* 453

L

La Boi Press
B *1:* 163
Labor/hard work, emphasis on
A *2:* 460
Laches (Plato)
B *2:* 315
Lakota culture, preserving
PS 34
Lakota people, religion of
B *1:* 56
Lakshmi (goddess)
A *2:* 244, 259, 260, 262
Lamashtu (demon)
A *1:* 60
Lamb symbol
A *1:* 138
Lan Caihe (god)
A *1:* 190
Landvaettir (spirits)
A *2:* 378
Langar function
A *2:* 433
Lao Laizi. *See* Laozi
Lao Tzu. *See* Laozi
Laos, religious tradition in
A *1:* 94
Lao-tse. *See* Laozi
Laozi
A *1:* 181 (ill.)
B *2:* **203–09,** 203 (ill.)
about
A *1:* 183
birth of
A *1:* 177–78
birthday celebrated
A *1:* 196
meeting with Confucius
B *2:* 204–06
origin
B *2:* 204
teachings of
A *1:* 154
travels

B *2:* 206
Las Navas de Tolosa, battle of
A *2:* 296
Lassalle, Ferdinand
B *2:* 263
Last Supper
A *1:* 122, 124, 131 (ill.),
140 (ill.)
Last Supper (da Vinci)
A *1:* 148
Lavater, Johann Kaspar
B *2:* 271–72
"Law" concept
A *2:* 355
PS 11
Laws (Plato)
B *2:* 315
Lay Missionaries of Charity
B *2:* 354
Leadership disputes, in Bahá'í faith
A *1:* 76–77
League of Militant Atheists
PS 200
Leap of faith
A *1:* 14–15
Legalist School
A *1:* 154
Leibowitz, Nechama
B *2:* **211–16**
Leibowitz, Yeshayahu
B *2:* 212
Lenaea
A *1:* 15
Lenin, Vladimir
B *2:* 268 (ill.)
Lent
A *1:* 140
Lesotho (South Africa)
B *2:* 369–70
Lessing, Gotthold
B *2:* 268–269, 274
Levi (son of Jacob)
B *1:* 6
Leviticus
B *2:* 283
See also Torah

Lhama Dhondup. *See* Dalai Lama
Lhasa, pilgrimages to
  A *1:* 110
Li (Confucian concept)
  B *1:* 86–87
Li Dan. *See* Laozi
Li Er. *See* Laozi
Li Po (Li Bai)
  A *1:* 204–05
Li principle
  A *1:* 161–62, 169, 174
Li Tieguai (god)
  A *1:* 190, 193
Li Yuan
  A *1:* 181
Li Zi
  A *1:* 191
Liebniz, Gottfried
  B *2:* 269
Life after death, belief in
  PS 24
The Life of Christ
  B *2:* 218
Liji (Li-chi)
  A *1:* 163
Literature, Muslim contributions
  to
  A *2:* 316–17, 319–20
Little Big Horn, Battle of
  B *1:* 53–54
"Lives of the Perfected" (Li Po)
  A *1:* 205
Lives of the Philosophers
  (Diogenes)
  B *2:* 312
Living, realm of
  PS 20
Logos (Divine Mind)
  A *1:* 219
Long Obligatory Prayer
  A *1:* 83
Lord Gouranga. *See* Chaitanya
  Mahaprabhu
Lord Lao. *See* Laozi
Lord Rama
  A *2:* 259–60

Lord Yama
  A *2:* 260
"The Lord's Prayer"
  A *1:* 139
  PS 205
Lord's Supper
  A *1:* 138
Lot
  B *1:* 3, 5, 6
Lotus Sutra
  A *1:* 100
  B *2:* 294, 296, 298, 299
Lotus symbolism
  B *2:* 313
Lourdes, pilgrimages to
  A *1:* 141
The Lovers of Meher Baba
  movement
  A *2:* 450
Loyalty (zhong)
  A *1:* 154
Loyola, Ignatius of
  B *2:* **217–23,** 217 (ill.)
  imprisonment
  B *2:* 220
  readings
  B *2:* 218
  travels
  B *2:* 219–20
Lu, duke of
  PS 128
Lu Dongbini (god)
  A *1:* 190, 193
Lu Tieguai (god)
  A *1:* 190
Lucianus, Martianus.
  See Calvin, John
Lucretius. *See On the Nature of*
  Things (Lucretius)
Lugh
  A *2:* 380
Lughnasad (Lughnasadh/Lamma)
  A *2:* 381
Lughnasadh festival
  A *2:* 389
Lukumi. *See* Santería

Lumbini, Nepal
  A *1:* 108–10
Lun Yu. *See* The Analects of
  Confucius
Lunar calendar
  A *1:* 107
Lupercalia festival
  A *1:* 233
Lupercus (god)
  A *1:* 233
Luther, Martin
  A *1:* 129, 133
  B *2:* **225–34,** 225 (ill.),
    226 (ill.)
  early life
  B *2:* 224
  excommunication
  B *2:* 230
  impact of
  B *2:* 233–34
  influence on Calvin
  B *1:* 76
  "justification through faith"
    doctrine
  B *2:* 303
  religious training
  B *2:* 226–27
  writings
  B *2:* 231
Lyceum
  A *1:* 217
Lyell, Charles
  A *1:* 29
Lysis (Plato)
  B *2:* 315

M

M. K. Gandhi. *See* Gandhi,
  Mahatma
Maat
  A *1:* 47, 61
Ma'ariv prayer
  A *2:* 359
Mabon
  A *2:* 389

Maccabee, Judah
  A *2:* 364
Madhva
  B *2:* **235–40**
  duelist philosophy
  B *2:* 338
  early life
  B *2:* 235–37
  similarities to Jesus Christ
  B *2:* 236–37
  studies
  B *2:* 237
  travels
  B *2:* 237, 238
Madhvacharya (Sri).
  See Madhva
Madhyamaka. *See* "Middle way"
Madinat al-Nadi
  A *2:* 294
Magen David symbol
  A *2:* 356–57, 357 (ill.)
Maggid
  A *2:* 362
Magha Puja Day (Sangha Day)
  A *1:* 108
Maghi holiday
  A *2:* 436
Magi
  A *2:* 447
Magi biblical story
  B *2:* 403
Magic wand
  A *2:* 387
Mah Nishtanah (Four Questions)
  A *2:* 362
Maha Bodhi Journal
  B *1:* 111
Maha Bodhi Society
  B *1:* 110
Maha Kumbh Mela
  A *2:* 260
Maha Maya
  A *1:* 87
Mahabba
  B *1:* 13
Mahabodhi Temple

  B *1:* 110
Mahabharata
  A *2:* 242, 253, 265
Maharaja Prataparudra
  B *2:* 241
Mahatma Gandhi.
  See Gandhi, Mohandas K.
Mahavira
  A *2:* 328 (ill.)
  B *2:* **241–47,** 242
  early life
  B *2:* 241–42
  Five Great Vows and
  A *2:* 327
  Jainism and
  A *2:* 323
  life of
  A *2:* 326–27
  PS 139–40
  teachings of
  A *2:* 328
  B *2:* 246–47
  travels
  B *2:* 243–44
  vows of
  PS 137–38, 145
  See also Jainism
Mahayana Buddhism
  A *1:* 90, 92, 94–95, 99
  B *1:* 73–74; *2:* 308, 312
  PS 172
Mahdi
  B *1:* 43, 380
Maiden from God
  A *1:* 71
Maidyarem festival
  A *2:* 458
Maidyoshahem festival
  A *2:* 457
Maidyozarem festival
  A *2:* 457
Maimonides, Moses
  A *2:* 352, 354
  B *2:* **249–56,** 249 (ill.)
  early life and travels
  B *2:* 249–51

education
  B *2:* 249–50
  influence of
  B *2:* 256
Maitreya (Laughing Buddha)
  A *1:* 103
Majalis-i Sab-a (Rūmī)
  B *1:* 183
Majushi
  A *1:* 103
Makaya Vodou
  A *2:* 281
Makharji, Kasturbai
  B *1:* 130
Mala beads
  A *2:* 257
Malcolm X
  A *2:* 300
Male-based religions
  A *1:* 7
Maliki legal tradition
  PS 30
Malkin, John
  B *2:* 360
Mandalas
  A *1:* 95, 102
"Mandate of Heaven"
  B *1:* 85–86
Mandela, Nelson
  B *2:* 373
Mangala Sutra
  A *1:* 112–13
Manipulation
  A *1:* 5
Mansion of Bahji
  A *1:* 82
Mantras
  in Nichiren Buddhism
  A *1:* 99
  in Vajrayana Buddhism
  A *1:* 95
Manuscript arts, Buddhist influence on
  A *1:* 115
Mao Shan (Mount Mao) sect
  A *1:* 185, 205

Mao Tse-tung. *See* Mao Zedong
Mao Zedong
   A *1:* 159, 182
Mara (the Evil One)
   PS 167, 169
Marathon, battle of
   A *1:* 211
Marcus Aurelius
   A *1:* 218
Marduk (Babylonian god)
   A *1:* 38, 41, 42, 45, 61
   B *1:* 2
   PS 11
   See also Festivals
Marfan's syndrome
   B *1:* 11
Marguerite of Navarre
   B *1:* 77
Marriage
   ancient Egypt
   A *1:* 63
   Baháʾí
   A *1:* 83
   Buddhist
   A *1:* 112–13
   Christian
   A *1:* 138
   Confucianist
   A *1:* 171
   Mesopotamian
   A *1:* 60
Marriage sacrament
   A *1:* 138
Mars
   A *1:* 122
Martyrdom of the Bab holiday
   A *1:* 82
Marx, Karl
   A *1:* 27, 31, 31 (ill.), 32
   B *2:* **257–65,** 257 (ill.),
      262 (ill.)
   early life
   B *2:* 258
   English years of
   B *2:* 261–63
   health problems
   B *2:* 263

occupations of
   B *2:* 259, 260
religious views
   B *2:* 264
travels
   B *2:* 260–61
   See also Engels, Friedrich
Marxism
   A *1:* 27
Mary (mother of Jesus Christ)
   A *1:* 7
   B *1:* 190, 192 (ill.);
      2: 219 (ill.)
Masada
   A *2:* 351
Masculine and feminine
   principles, in creation myths
   PS 3
Masekhtots (tractates)
   A *2:* 356
Mashriquʾl-Adhkar
   (Houses of Worship)
   A *1:* 80–81
Masnavi (Rumi)
   A *2:* 319
   B *1:* 182, 183
Masterless samurai
   A *1:* 173
Materialism
   A *1:* 23, 24, 26
   B *2:* 264
   See also Atheism; Huxley,
      Thomas Henry
Mathematics, and ancient religions
   A *1:* 65
Mathura (city)
   A *2:* 260
Mattathias the Hasmonean
   A *2:* 364
Matthew 6: **A** *1:* 14–15, 121
Matthew 22: **A** *1:* 37–40, 121
Matthew, Saint
   about
   PS 211
   gospels of
   PS 207–11

Maturation rituals,
   in Confucianiam
   A *1:* 170–71
Matzo
   A *2:* 362
Maysara
   B *1:* 198
Mazdayasna
   A *2:* 443
Mazdaznan Movement
   A *2:* 450
Mazzolini, Sylvester
   B *2:* 229
McKinley, William, assassination
   attempt on
   PS 201
The Meaning of Witchcraft
   (Gardner)
   B *1:* 141
Mecca
   B *1:* 195–96; *2:* 300 (ill.)
   Abraham and
   A *2:* 315
   conquering of
   A *2:* 294
   idol worship in
   A *2:* 292
   pilgrimages to
   A *2:* 315–16
Meccan revelations
   B *2:* 289
Meccan suras
   A *2:* 307
Medical treatises
   A *2:* 265
Medicine, Daoism and
   A *1:* 201–02
Medieval Period of Hinduism
   A *2:* 241
Medina
   A *2:* 294
Medinan revelations
   A *2:* 307
Meditation
   A *1:* 107 (ill.)
   B *1:* 116

basic forms of
A *1:* 104
Confucianism
A *1:* 167
Daoism
A *1:* 194
exercises
A *1:* 198–200
as means to enlightenment
A *1:* 99, 103–04
See also Dipa Ma; Vipassana
meditation; Yoga
Meditation mudra
A *1:* 109
Meditations (Aurelius)
A *1:* 218, 229
Medium Obligatory Prayer
A *1:* 83
Medzhibozh (Podolia)
B *1:* 177
Meher Baba
A *2:* 450
Meiji Restoration
A *2:* 396
Melchior (magi)
B *2:* 403
Meme theory
A *1:* 12–13, 13 (ill.)
Memphis
A *1:* 44
Men of Poland and Austria
B *1:* 176
Menassah (grandson of Jacob)
B *1:* 6
Mencius (Confucius)
B *1:* 88
See also Mengzi
Mendelssohn, Moses
B *2:* **267–75,** 267 (ill.)
early years
B *2:* 268–69
legacy of
B *2:* 274
views on mysticism
B *2:* 271
writings of
B *2:* 269, 271, 272–73

Menes. *See* Mengzi
Menexenus (Plato)
B *2:* 316
Meng Tzu. *See* Mengzi
Mengzi
A *1:* 41, 155, 159–60, 163
Meno (Plato)
B *2:* 316
Menorah
A *2:* 358, 364
See also Hanukkah
(Chanukah) festival
Mercury
A *1:* 122
*The Merging of Spirit and
Science* (Einstein)
A *1:* 116
"Merit vows," of Jains
A *2:* 340–41
Mesopotamia
B *1:* 2, 121–22
about
A *1:* 39
architectural remains of
A *1:* 51–52
creation story of
A *1:* 48–49
environment of
A *1:* 39–40
festivals
A *1:* 42, 60
gods of
A *1:* 61
mathematics and science
A *1:* 65
religion in
A *1:* 8, 37, 56–57
role of priests in
A *1:* 52–53, 55
writing system of
A *1:* 65
See also Babylonians; Egypt
Mesopotamian religion
A *1:* 8, 42
Messiah, described
A *1:* 121

Messiah, Jewish belief in
PS 203
Metamorphoses (Ovid)
A *1:* 211, 238–39
Metaphysics (Aristotle)
A *1:* 229
B *1:* 39
Metempsychosis belief
A *1:* 214
Methodism
A *1:* 134
Mevlana Mausoleum (Turkey)
B *1:* 183 (ill.)
Mezuzah symbol
A *2:* 358–59
Michelangelo
A *1:* 147–48
Michkat al-Anwar (Corner for
Lights) (al-Ghazālī)
B *1:* 149–50
Micius
A *1:* 155
Middle Kingdom (Egypt)
A *1:* 44
"Middle way"
A *1:* 88–89, 90
B *1:* 70
Midsummer's Day
A *2:* 380 (ill.)
Mika'il (angel)
A *2:* 309
Milesian School
A *1:* 208, 213
B *1:* 26
Miletus
B *1:* 26
Military draft, opposition to
PS 195
Minchah service
A *2:* 359
Mind, nature of
PS 167
"Mindfulness"
B *1:* 119; *2:* 363
Minerva
A *1:* 122

Minhag Amerika (Wise)
B *2:* 394
Ministery of Divinities
A *2:* 298
Ministry of Religion
A *2:* 398
Minoans. *See* Crete
Miracles
A *1:* 10–11
B *2:* 287
Miraj of Muhammad
B *2:* 303
Miri symbol
A *2:* 432
Miriam, (sister of Moses)
B *2:* 285
Mirrors, symbolism of
A *2:* 407
Mirza ꞌAli Nuri, Husayn
A *1:* 71
Mirza Yahya
B *1:* 54–55
See also Baháꞌuꞌlláh
Mishnah
B *2:* 252 (ill.), 254
Mishneh Torah (Maimonides)
A *2:* 354, 356
B *2:* 255–56
Missionaries of Charity
B *2:* 292–94
Missionaries of Charity Brothers
B *2:* 293–94
Missionary work
A *1:* 146–47
Mithra (god)
A *1:* 220
symbol of
A *1:* 230
Mithraism
A *2:* 447
Mithraism mystery cult
A *1:* 220
Mittelbau-Dora concentration camp
B *2:* 364
Mo Tzu
A *1:* 155

Moderation
A *1:* 16, 187
Modern Neo-Idealistic
Confucianism
A *1:* 160
Modern Neo-Rationalistic
Confucianism
A *1:* 160
Modern Period of Hinduism
A *2:* 241, 242
Moꞌed (Festival)
A *2:* 356
Mohammad. *See* Muhammad
Mohandas Gandhi. *See* Gandhi,
Mahatma
Mohandas Karamchand Gandhi.
See Gandhi, Mahatma
Mohomet. *See* Muhammad
Moksha (moksa)
A *2:* 248
See also Salvation
Moksha, defined
PS 146
Momaday, N. Scott
B *1:* 57
Monastary visits
A *1:* 111
Monastic law
A *1:* 99–100
Monetary practices, of Muslims
A *2:* 315
Mongol invasions
B *1:* 168
Mongolia, religious tradition in
A *1:* 95
Monism
A *1:* 226
B *2:* 237, 338
Monks and monasteries
A *1:* 126
See also Daoism
Monotheism
in Baháꞌí
PS 175–76
concept of
A *1:* 25

creation myths of
PS 1–2
defined
B *1:* 196
development of
B *1:* 2
in Egypt
B *1:* 9, 12
in India
B *2:* 239
Moses and
B *2:* 284
Muhammad and
B *2:* 302
New Kingdom period
A *1:* 44–45
in Qurꞌan
PS 23
Roman Empire
A *1:* 212
Sankara and
B *2:* 338
Sikhism
A *2:* 419, 427
PS 85
in Tanakh
PS 6
Zarathushtra and
B *2:* 399
Zoroastrianism
A *2:* 443
Moon crescent symbol
A *2:* 334
Moors
A *1:* 127
See also Islam
Moral codes
in African indigenous
religions
A *2:* 275
commonality of in religions
A *1:* 11–12
religion's role in
A *1:* 16
Morgan (god)
A *2:* 380

Morning Hours; or, Lectures about God's Existence (Mendelssohn)
  B *2:* 274
Moses
  A *1:* 4; *2:* 346
  B *2:* **277–84,** 277 (ill.), 282 (ill.)
  PS 24
  early life
  B *2:* 279–80
  God's task for
  B *2:* 280
  influences on
  B *1:* 12–13
  parting words of
  B *2:* 284
  receives the Ten Commandments
  B *2:* 278
  Sinai Peninsula refuge
  B *2:* 280
  See also Israelites
Moses (movie)
  A *2:* 368
Moses and Monotheism (Freud)
  B *1:* 13
Moshe ben Maimon. *See* Maimonides, Moses
Motammem Al-Bayan
  B *1:* 54
"Mother Earth Bulletin"
  PS 199 (ill.)
Mother Earth journal
  PS 193
Mother Goddess
  worship of
  A *1:* 6–7
  See also Venus of Willendorf
Mother Teresa. *See* Teresa, Mother
Mount Ano San. *See* Ano San, Mount
Mount Arafat. *See* Arafat, Mount
Mount Fuji. *See* Fuji, Mount
Mount Girnar. *See* Girnar, Mount
Mount Hira. *See* Hira, Mount

Mount Nantai Shan. *See* Nantai Shan, Mount
Mount Olympus (Greece). *See* Olympus, Mount (Greece)
Mozi
  A *1:* 155
Muawiya
  B *1:* 30
Mudras
  about
  A *1:* 109
  See also specific mudras
Muezzin
  A *2:* 312
Muggeridge, Malcolm
  B *2:* 294
Muhammad
  B *2:* **285–92**
  Abraham
  B *1:* 8
  'Ali ibn Abī Tālīb
  B *1:* 17, 18
  Bani Hashim clan
  B *1:* 196
  death and ascent of
  A *2:* 294
  early life
  B *2:* 87
  family of
  B *2:* 197, 287, 292
  hijrah
  B *2:* 289
  influence on Usuman Dan Fodio
  B *2:* 379
  successor to
  A *2:* 298
  travels
  B *1:* 201–02
  view of in Islam
  A *1:* 4
  visions and revelations
  B *1:* 200–01; *2:* 289
  See also Fatima (daughter of Muhammad); Khadijah
  visitation from Jabra'il

  A *2:* 292–93
Muhammad Ahmad
  B *2:* 380
Muhammad Ali
  A *2:* 300
Muhammad, Qur'an revealed to
  PS 23
Muktad festival
  A *2:* 458
Mula Sankara. *See* Dayananda Sarasvati
Mulamadhya-maka-Karika
  A *1:* 101
Mulk, Nizam Al-
  B *1:* 147
Mummification
  A *1:* 58
Mumon-kan (Gateless Gate)
  A *1:* 100
Munkidh min al-Dalal Al- (Al-Ghazālī)
  B *1:* 146
Muqaddima (Introduction) (ibn Khaldūn)
  B *1:* 163, 166–67
Murray, Margaret
  B *1:* 141
Murti
  A *2:* 257
Museum of Magic and Witchcraft
  B *1:* 140
Music, influence of Christianity on
  A *1:* 148
Music and dance
  A *1:* 174
Muslim, empire of
  A *2:* 294–96, 297–98
Muslim countries, colonization of
  A *2:* 299–300
Muslims
  core beliefs of
  PS 23–24
  legal traditions of
  PS 30

similarity to beliefs of Jews
and Christians
PS 30
Myohorengekyo. *See* Lotus Sutra
Myoto-Iwa
A *2:* 406 (ill.)
Mystery cults
A *1:* 224–26
Mystery of life's meaning
A *2:* 288
Mythical themes
A *1:* 236
Myths
A *1:* 8, 13–14
Myths, as fundamental truth
PS 1

N

Naam Karam ceremony
A *2:* 435
Nagarjuna
A *1:* 101
Nahor (brother of Abraham)
B *1:* 2
Naimittika rituals
A *2:* 258
Namaskar prayer
A *2:* 335
"Namaste" custom
A *2:* 265
Namdari group
A *2:* 426
Naming rituals, in Buddhism
A *1:* 112
Namokar Mantra
A *2:* 335
Nanak Dev
B *1:* 153–54
Nanak Dev Ji, Guru
A *2:* 419, 425 (ill.)
Nanak Dev Ji, Sri Guru
PS 85, 86
Nanna (god)
A *1:* 40, 47, 60
B *1:* 122

Nanna Ziggurat
A *1:* 57
Nantai Shan, Mount
A *2:* 413
Naphtali (son of Jacob)
B *1:* 6
Naram-Sin
A *1:* 40
Narendra Nath Datta.
See Vivekananda, Swami
Nashik (city)
A *2:* 260
Nashim (Women)
A *2:* 356
Nasrid Muhammad V
B *1:* 171
Nataputta Vardhamana.
See Mahavira
Nathan the Wise (Lessing)
B *2:* 267
National Confucian Academy
A *1:* 166
Native American nature spirits
A *2:* 410
Native American religion
A *2:* 285–89
overview
A *2:* 285–86
See also specific tribes
Natural forces, deities based on
A *1:* 5
"Natural selection"
A *1:* 15, 34
Nature gods, worship of
A *1:* 42
Nature spirits
A *2:* 277
Navjote Ceremony
A *2:* 460
Navratri festival
A *2:* 260
Navvab, Asiyih
B *1:* 43
Nawfal, Waraqah Ibn
B *1:* 196, 199
Naw-Ruz festival
A *1:* 81–82

Nazi invasion of Poland
B *2:* 262–63
Nazi Party, and Asatru
A *2:* 377
Nazi regime. *See* Swastika symbol
Neanderthals
A *1:* 4–5
Near to Correctness
A *1:* 164
Nebuchadnezzar (king)
A *2:* 346
Nefertiti
B *1:* 10
Nehru, Jawaharlal
A *2:* 424–25
B *1:* 134
Nehru Prize
B *2:* 294
Neihardt, John G.
B *1:* 57
Neith (god)
A *1:* 45
Nemi/Neminatha
A *2:* 339
Neo-Confucianism
A *1:* 157, 160
Neo-Daoism
A *1:* 184
Neo-Paganism
A *2:* **371–91**
PS 97
about
A *2:* 375
characteristics of
A *2:* 373–76
nature and structure of
A *2:* 374
overview
A *2:* 371–73
rituals of
A *2:* 375
See also Wiccans
Neoplatonism
A *1:* 219, 236
Nepal, religious tradition in
A *1:* 95

Nephtys (god)
  A *1:* 43
Neptune
  A *1:* 122
Neue Rheinische Zeitung newspaper
  B *2:* 267
Nevi'im
  PS 5
Nevi'im, books of
  A *2:* 354
New American Cyclopedia (Marx)
  B *2:* 268–69
New Confucianism
  A *1:* 160
New Confucians
  A *1:* 175
New England transcendentalists
  A *1:* 93
New Kingdom
  A *1:* 44
New Life movement
  A *1:* 181–82
New Testament
  A *1:* 136–37
  PS 203
New Text School of
  Confucianism
  A *1:* 160
New Year's Festival
  A *1:* 57, 107; *2:* 422
New York Daily Tribune
  B *2:* 268
Newton, Isaac
  A *1:* 26
Nezikin (Damages)
  A *2:* 356
Nicene Creed
  A *1:* 127, 131–32
Nichiren
  B *2:* **293–300**
  after World War II
  B *2:* 299–300
  early life
  B *2:* 293–94
  exile
  B *2:* 295–96

ordination
  B *2:* 294
posthumous honors
  B *2:* 296
Nichiren Buddhism
  A *1:* 92, 99
Nicomachean Ethics (Aristotle)
  B *1:* 39–40
Nietzsche, Friedrich
  A *1:* 15, 27–28
Nihangs sect
  A *2:* 426
Nihonshoki
  PS 21
Nihonshoki text
  A *2:* 396, 406
Nile River area, rise of religion in
  A *1:* 8
Nimai. *See* Caitanya Mahaprabhu
"Nine Noble Virtues" of Asatru
  A *2:* 377
Nineteen-Day Feast Bahá'í
  A *1:* 82
Ninety-five theses (Luther)
  A *1:* 129
  B *2:* 226–28, 230 (ill.)
Nineveh, winged bull sculptures
  at
  A *1:* 51
Ninhursag (goddess)
  A *1:* 47
Nin-hursag (mother goddess)
  A *1:* 47
Nin-me-sar-ra (Queen of Count-
  less Divine Powers)
  B *1:* 125
Ninna/Sin (god)
  A *1:* 37, 47
Nippur
  A *1:* 42
Nirankaris group
  A *2:* 426
Nirmal Hriday hospice
  B *2:* 295 (ill.)
Nirmalas sect
  A *2:* 426

Nirvana
  B *1:* 61, 74
Nirvana, explained
  PS 166
Nirvana concept
  A *1:* 23, 89–90
Nishan Sahib flag
  A *2:* 432
Nit (god)
  A *1:* 43
Nitya rituals
  A *2:* 258
Nityananda
  B *2:* 240 (ill.)
Nivritti
  A *2:* 248
Noah
  B *1:* 3
Nobel Peace Prize
  A *2:* 367
  B *2:* 294
Nobel Prizes
  A *2:* 366–67
Nonaction, emphasis on in Daoism
  PS 150
Nonharmful karma,
  Jain concept of
  A *2:* 332
Non-*jiva* (soul), divisions of
  PS 138
"Nonreligious" census category
  A *1:* 21
  See also Atheism
Non-violent protest
  B *1:* 133, 134
Nordisk sed
  A *2:* 376
Norse heathenism
  A *2:* 376
North America, Mother
  Goddess in
  A *1:* 7
Northern Buddhism.
  See Mahayana Buddhism
"Northern School"
  A *2:* 244

Northern School of Buddhism
PS 172

Norway, non-believers in
A 1: 31

Nothingness, emphasis on in Daoism
PS 150

Notre Dame cathedral
A 1: 141

Nous. See Anaxagoras

Numbers. See Torah

Numbers (Bible)
B 2: 289

Nuri, Mirza Abbas
B 1: 41

Nuri, Mirza Husayn 'Ali
B 1: 41–49
break with Islam
B 1: 44
imprisonment and exile
B 1: 45
public declaration by
B 1: 46

Nut (god)
A 1: 43

Nyaya
B 1: 68–69

Nyx and Eros
PS 32

O No Yasumaro
A 2: 405
PS 14

Obatala
A 2: 285

The Obscenities of the Esoterics (Al-Ghazālī)
B 1: 148

"Obstructing" karma
A 2: 332

Ocha. See Santería

Odin (god)
A 2: 377

Odinism
A 2: 376

The Odyssey (Homer)
A 1: 210, 228
PS 73–84

Of Water and the Spirit (Somé)
B 2: 370–71

Offering ceremonies
A 1: 166

Offering of Eightfold Puja
A 2: 337–38

Oggzn (orisha), renaming of
A 2: 283

Oglala Sioux
A 2: 287
PS 3, 35 (ill.)

Olcott, Colonel Henry Steel
B 1: 109

Olcott, Henry S.
A 1: 102

Old Kingdom (Egypt)
A 1: 44

Old Testament
A 1: 136
PS 203
See also Tanakh (Torah)

Old Text School, of Confucianism
A 1: 160

Old Way
A 2: 376

Olmo Lungring
A 2: 289

Olódùmarè
A 2: 283

Olympus, Mount (Greece)
A 1: 220–22

Om mani padme hum mantra
A 1: 104

Om symbol
A 2: 335, 335 (ill.)

On Nature (Anaxagoras)
B 1: 27

On Nature (Parmenides)
A 1: 229

On the Civil Amelioration of the

Condition of the Jews (Mendelssohn)
B 2: 279

On the Jewish Question (Marx)
B 2: 266

On the Nature of Things (Lucretius)
A 1: 31–32

On the Origin of Species (Darwin)
A 1: 15, 34

Oneness, in Bahá'í faith
A 1: 77

Onokoro island
PS 17

An Open Heart: Practicing Compassion in Everyday Life (Dalai Lama)
B 1: 97

Opet festival
A 1: 57–58

"Opium of the people" (Marx)
A 1: 32

Oracle of Delphi
A 1: 233–34

Oracles
A 1: 223, 231

Oral Torah. See Talmud

Order and chaos, fight between
A 1: 49

Order of Bards, Ovates, and Druids (OBOD)
A 2: 381

Ordo Templi Orientis
B 1: 140

The Oresteia (Aeschylus)
A 1: 211

Organized religion, development of in Egypt
A 1: 37

Organon (Aristotle)
B 1: 38–39

Organum (Aristotle)
A 1: 229

Origami
A 2: 416

*The Origin of Christianity, and a
    Commentary on the Acts of the
    Apostles* (Wise)
  B *2:* 397
Original Sin
  A *1:* 134, 236
Orishas
  A *2:* 282–83
Orpheus, journey to the underworld
  PS 21
Orphic mystery cults
  A *1:* 224, 225
Orthodox Bahá'í sect
  A *1:* 76–77
Othrodox Christianity, view of
    Jesus in
  A *1:* 3–4
Orthodox Judaism
  B *2:* 392, 394
Orthodox Judaism, beliefs of
  A *2:* 351–52
Orthodox Vodou
  A *2:* 280–81
Osiris (god)
  A *1:* 15, 38, 43, 44,
    46 (ill.), 148
  described
  A *1:* 61
Ostara (goddess)
  A *2:* 378, 388–89
Ouagadougou
  B *2:* 371
Ovates class
  A *2:* 379
Ovid
  A *1:* 211
Ox-Creator
  PS 189
Oyasama
  A *2:* 401

P

Pagan, interpretations of
  A *2:* 371–73

Paganism
  PS 101
  See also Wicca
Pahlavi language
  A *2:* 453
Paitishahem festival
  A *2:* 458
Palestine
  after the Crusades
  B *2:* 250
  Arabs in
  A *2:* 349–50
  Roman control of
  A *1:* 121–22
Pali Canon
  A *1:* 90, 99–100
  B *1:* 73
Panathenaea festival
  A *1:* 231, 233
Panchen Lama
  B *1:* 95
Panchendriya beings
  A *2:* 331
Pangu, emergence of
  PS 2
Pantheism
  A *1:* 214
Papal infallibility
  A *1:* 132–33
"Paper on Hinduism"
  PS 109–20
  about
  PS 109–10
  excerpts from
  PS 113–18
  See also Swami Vivekananda;
    World Parliament of
    Religions
Papyrus of Ani. *See* Book
  of the Dead
Parasparopagraho Jivanam text
  A *2:* 335
Parentalia festival
  A *1:* 235
Paris Commune
  B *2:* 269

Parmenides
  A *1:* 214, 226, 227
Parshva
  enlightenment of
  A *2:* 339
  Five Great Vows and
  A *2:* 327
Parsi Reform Movement
  A *2:* 449
Parsi Theosophy
  A *2:* 449–50
Parsi Zoroastrianism
  A *2:* 450
Parsis (Parsees)
  A *2:* 443
Parsvanath Hill
  A *2:* 339
Parvati (goddess)
  A *2:* 262
Paryushana holiday
  A *2:* 339
Passover (Pesach)
  A *1:* 122; *2:* 361–62
Passover feast
  B *2:* 287
Patent of Toleration
  B *2:* 280
Pateti holiday
  A *2:* 458, 458 (ill.)
Path of Judgment
  (Chinvat Peretum)
  A *2:* 452
Patron gods of cities
  A *1:* 223
Pattabhi Jois, Sri K.
  A *2:* 267
Paul (Saint)
  A *1:* 123, 236
  B *2:* **301–09**, 301 (ill.), 305 (ill.)
  conversion to Christianity
  B *2:* 304
  early life
  B *2:* 302–04
  Epistles written by
  B *2:* 302
  travels

B *2:* 304–05, 306–07, 308
See also Council of Jerusalem
Pauline Christianity
    B *2:* 301, 307–08, 315
Pauline epistles
    A *1:* 137
    See also Paul, Saint
Peasant's War of 1524–25
    B *2:* 231
Pedro the Cruel
    B *1:* 165
Peloponnesian War
    A *1:* 211
    B *2:* 313
Penance sacrament
    A *1:* 139
Pensées philosophiques (Diderot)
    A *1:* 26
Pentacle
    A *2:* 387 (ill.), 388
Pentagrams, symbolism of
    PS 101–02
"The people of the Book," respect
    for
    A *2:* 298–99
People's Republic of China
    A *1:* 182
People's Republic of China, effect
    on Daoism
    PS 161–62
"Perception-obscuring" karma
    A *2:* 332
Perfect and Great Way sect
    A *1:* 185
"Perfection of Wisdom" sutras
    A *1:* 100
Perfectionism, and Original Sin
    A *1:* 134
Pericles
    B *1:* 27, 29, 35
Period of the One Hundred
    Schools
    A *1:* 155
Perry, Matthew
    A *2:* 396
Persephone
    A *1:* 224

Persian Empire
    B *2:* 313, 405
Persian Sassanid Dynasty
    A *2:* 448
Persian Wars
    A *1:* 211
Perumal, Ilaya. *See* Ramanuja
Peter (apostle)
    A *1:* 121
Phädon (Mendelssohn)
    B *2:* 277
Phaedo (Plato)
    A *1:* 229
    B *2:* 316
Phaedrus (Plato)
    B *2:* 316
Pharaoh
    as living god
    A *1:* 47
    power of
    A *1:* 44
Pharisee
    B *2:* 302, 316
Pharisees
    A *2:* 350
Philebus (Plato)
    B *2:* 317, 331
Philip II of Madedon
    A *1:* 211
Philosophical Conversions
    (Mendelssohn)
    B *2:* 275
Philosophical Daoism *vs.* religious
    Daoism
    A *1:* 182–83
"Philosophical Thoughts"
    (Diderot)
    A *1:* 26
"The Philosophy of Atheism"
    PS 123, **193–202**
    See also Atheism; Atheists;
        Atheists United
Phowa prayer
    A *1:* 113
Physical universe, creation of
    PS 23

Physics
    basic law of
    A *1:* 215
    Empedocles and
    A *1:* 237
Physics (Aristotle)
    A *1:* 229
    B *1:* 39
Pilgrimages
    A *1:* 11
    Bahá'í destination for
    A *1:* 82
    Buddhist
    A *1:* 108–11
    Christian
    A *1:* 140–41
    Confucian
    A *1:* 169
    Daoist
    A *1:* 197–98
    Greek Orthodox
    A *1:* 233–34
    Islam
    A *2:* 306, 314–16
    Jain
    A *2:* 339–40
    Japanese
    A *2:* 412–13
    Jewish
    A *1:* 141
    to Mecca
    B *2:* 301
    Zoroastrian
    A *2:* 459
"Pillars of Islam"
    A *2:* 305–06
Pine Ridge Reservation
    B *1:* 54 (ill.)
Pir-e Banu-Pars shrine
    A *2:* 459
Pir-e Herisht shrine
    A *2:* 459
Pir-e Naraki shrine
    A *2:* 459
Pir-e Narestuneh shrine
    A *2:* 459

Pir-e-Sabz shrine
  A *2:* 459
Piri symbol
  A *2:* 432
Pitriloka
  A *2:* 256
Pitta (digestion energy)
  A *2:* 268
Pittsburgh Platform document
  B *2:* 395
Plagues, on Egypt
  B *2:* 287–88
"Plant-bodied" beings
  A *2:* 330
Plato
  A *1:* 216, 217 (ill.), 226
  B *2:* **311–18,** 315 (ill.)
  imprisonment
  B *2:* 316–17
  travels
  B *2:* 314–16
  tutor of Dion
  B *2:* 315
  See also Allegory of the Cave
    (Plato); Socrates
Platonic Love
  B *2:* 312
Plotinus
  A *1:* 219
Plum Village (France)
  B *2:* 363
Pluto
  A *1:* 122
Podolia, Judaism in
  B *1:* 172–73, 177
Poetics (Aristotle)
  B *1:* 39
Poetry, knowledge of
  A *1:* 174
Pogroms
  B *1:* 172
Polish Ukraine Jewish
  population
  B *1:* 172–73
Politics (Aristotle)
  B *1:* 35, 39

Polytheism
  B *1:* 196
  ancient Egypt
  A *1:* 38
  ancient Greece and Rome
  A *1:* 207–08
  ancient Mesopotamia
  A *1:* 37–38
  Asatru
  A *2:* 377
  Daoism
  A *1:* 188–89
  Druidism
  A *2:* 380–82
Pope John XXIII Peace Prize
  B *2:* 294
Poruwa Ceremony
  A *1:* 112
Poseidon
  A *1:* 222, 223
The Poverty of Philosophy (Marx)
  B *2:* 266
Power, of Wiccans
  PS 100
The Power and the Glory (Greene)
  A *1:* 147
Prajnaparamita
  A *1:* 100
Prakash Utsav holiday
  A *2:* 436
Prarabdha Karma
  A *2:* 263
Pravritti
  A *2:* 248
Prayag (city)
  A *2:* 260
Prayer beads
  A *2:* 257
"Prayer of Judith"
  A *2:* 368–69
Prayer wheel, in Tibetan
  Buddhism
  A *1:* 11
Prayers
  Greeks and Roman
  A *1:* 231

Jewish
  A *1:* 359–61
  Zoroastrian
  A *2:* 455–56
Predestination
  A *1:* 75, 133–34
Presidency College
  B *2:* 384
Pretoria Bantu Normal College
  B *2:* 377
Priestesses, duties
  B *1:* 125
Priestesses of Greece
  A *1:* 231
Priests of Egypt
  A *1:* 45
Priests of Mesopotamia
  A *1:* 53, 56 (ill.)
Primary element, names for
  A *1:* 213
Princess Mirabai
  A *2:* 265
"The Princess of Mecca"
  B *1:* 195
"The Princess of Quraysh"
  B *1:* 195
Principles of Communism (Engles)
  B *2:* 267
*Principles of the Philosophy of the
  Future* (Feuerbach)
  A *1:* 32
The Prophet. *See* Muhammad
Prophets. *See* Nevi'im
Protagoras (Plato)
  A *1:* 24, 215
  B *2:* 315
Protestant Reformation
  B *2:* 227–28, 303, 317
Protestantism
  A *1:* 129–30, 133–34
Protestantism, development of
  B *2:* 229
Proverbs
  PS 5
Psalms
  PS 5

Psyche/soul, belief in
    A *1:* 223
Psychotherapy, and Buddhist
    principles
    A *1:* 115–16
Ptah (god)
    A *1:* 41, 43, 44
Pu in Daoism
    A *1:* 187
Public rituals, at Confucian temples
    A *1:* 166
Puja (worship)
    A *2:* 256, 257–58, 259 (ill.)
Punjab region
    A *2:* 423
Punjabi language
    PS 88
Pure Land Buddhism
    A *1:* 95
    B *2:* 312
Pure Land Sutra
    A *1:* 100
"The Pure One"
    B *1:* 195
Purgatory
    A *1:* 144
Purification rituals of Shinto
    A *2:* 404
Puritanism
    A *1:* 134
Purnaprajna. *See* Madhva
Purple Heaven Temple,
    pilgrimages to
    A *1:* 198
Purusharthas
    A *2:* 248
Purva scripture group
    A *2:* 333
Pyramids
    A *1:* 52
Pyrrho of Elis
    A *1:* 219
Pythagoras
    A *1:* 214
    B *2:* 314, 328
    modern mathematics and

    A *1:* 237
Pythagorean Mysteries
    A *1:* 226
Pythian Games
    A *1:* 233
Pythias
    B *1:* 35

Q

Qadimi calendar
    A *2:* 457
Qasim (son of Muhammad)
    B *1:* 197
Qaysiyya, Rabi'a Al-. *See* Rābi'a
    al-Adawiyah
Qi (ch'i) concept
    A *1:* 187, 199
Qiguan Shi (Ch'i-kuan Shih)
    B *1:* 85
Qing (Ch'ing) Dynasty
    PS 160
Qing Dynasty, use of
    Confucianism by
    A *1:* 158
Quakers
    A *1:* 134
Quanzhen (Chuan Chen) sect
    A *1:* 185
Quests, in Apache tribal life
    A *2:* 289
Qufu
    A *1:* 169
Qui Kong. *See* Confucius
Qumran, Israel
    PS 11
Qur'an
    B *1:* 28; *2:* 302
    PS 23–31, 25 (ill.)
    after death of Muhammad
    PS 29
    creation account in
    PS 2
    described
    PS 24–25
    how to read

    PS 26
    revelation of
    A *2:* 306–07
    style of
    A *2:* 307
    translations of
    PS 25
    writing down
    A *2:* 308–09
Qur'an-e Farsi (Rumi)
    B *1:* 183
Qur'anic Muslims
    B *2:* 300
Quraysh tribe
    B *1:* 26, 27, 29–30, 194, 199;
    2: 301

R

Ra/Re (sun god)
    A *1:* 38, 43, 61
Rābi'a al-Adawiyah
    B *2:* **319–25**
    early life
    B *2:* 319–20
    religious practices
    B *2:* 320–21
    sainthood
    B *2:* 324
    travels
    B *2:* 323–24
Radkhani, Ahmad Al-
    B *1:* 146
Ra'kah
    A *2:* 313
Ram Das, Guru
    A *2:* 421, 436–37
    PS 86
Rama
    A *2:* 262
    See also Lord Rama
Ramadan
    A *2:* 313–14
Ramakrishna
    PS 111

Ramakrishna (Shri)
  B *2:* 385–86
Ramakrishna Math order
  B *2:* 389
Ramakrishna Mission
  B *2:* 389
  PS 118
Ramanuja
  A *2:* 244
  B *2:* **327–36**
  early life
  B *2:* 327–28
  writings of
  B *2:* 331–32
  See also Madhva;
    Yamunacharya
Ramayana
  A *2:* 265
  composition of
  A *2:* 242
Rambam, The.
  See Maimonides, Moses
Ramses II
  B *2:* 285
Ranjit Singh
  A *2:* 423
Rapithwin
  A *2:* 456
Rashidun
  B *1:* 31
Rastafarians, number of
  A *1:* 2
Rationalists
  A *1:* 226
Rationality, as highest good
  A *1:* 217
Ravensbrück concentration camp
  B *2:* 363 (ill.), 364
Realist School
  A *1:* 154
Reality, basis of
  A *1:* 226
Rebekah (wife of Isaac)
  B *1:* 7
Reclining Buddha
  A *1:* 114

Reconstructionist Judaism
  beliefs of
  A *2:* 352
  creator-god concept in
  A *1:* 20
"Record of Ancient Matters."
  See Kojiki text
Record of Rites (Confucius)
  A *1:* 163
  PS 136
Record of Rites ceremony
  A *1:* 166
Records of the Grand Historian
  (Sima Qian)
  PS 126
Recreation, in Mesopotamia
  A *1:* 60
Rectification of Names principle
  A *1:* 161
Red Cloud
  B *1:* 53
Red Sea, parting of
  B *2:* 288
Reform Bahá'í faith
  A *1:* 77
Reform Judaism
  B *2:* 280, 394, 395
  beliefs of
  A *2:* 352
Reformation
  A *1:* 25, 129
  See also Protestantism
Reformed Christianity.
  See Protestantism
Reformed Confucianism
  A *1:* 160
Reformed Druids of North
  America
  A *2:* 382
Reformers, of Protestantism
  A *1:* 133
Regeneration myths
  A *1:* 48
Regla de Ocha. *See* Santería
Rehit Maryada
  A *2:* 431

Reincarnation
  A *2:* 247–48, 332, 380
  PS 88, 110
Rei-sai festival
  A *2:* 411–12
Religion
  anthropological view of
  A *1:* 4
  definitions of
  A *1:* 1–2
  development of law due to
  A *1:* 16–17
  development of in
    Mesopotamia
  A *1:* 37
  history of practice of
  A *1:* 4–5
  neuroscientific view of
  A *1:* 12–13
  role of
  A *1:* 16–17
  theories on origin of
  A *1:* 3–6
  universality of
  A *1:* 2, 12–13
  See also specific religions
Religion and the state,
  separation of
  B *2:* 279–80
Religions
  alienation from
  A *2:* 296
  common traits of
  A *1:* 10–12
  number of
  A *1:* 8–9
  types of
  A *1:* 9–10
The Religions of Man (Smith)
  A *1:* 96, 119
Religions or cults
  A *1:* 10
Religious affiliation
  A *1:* 130
Religious atheism
  A *1:* 21–22

Religious Confucianism
  A *1:* 179
Religious Daoism
  A *1:* 179–81, 183
Religious extremists
  A *2:* 300–01
Religious festival
  PS 117 (ill.)
Religious festivals
  in ancient Egypt
  A *1:* 63–64
  in Greece and Rome
  A *1:* 231, 233
Religious laws
  A *1:* 16–17
Religious movements in
  Poland/Ukraine
  B *1:* 173
Religious philosophies, rise of
  A *1:* 8
Religious revivals
  PS 196
Religious Society of Friends
  A *1:* 134
Religious symbols
  A *1:* 3 (ill.)
  of Egypt and Mesopotamia
  A *1:* 42
Remey, Mason
  A *1:* 76
Ren concept
  PS 126
Ren principle
  A *1:* 160–61, 161 (ill.), 164–65
Rencho. *See* Nichiren
The Republic (Plato)
  A *1:* 216, 229
  B *2:* 316, 317–18
Research Institute of Prakrit,
  Ahimsa, and Jainology
  B *2:* 253
*Resignation and Fidelity, or Life
  and Romance* (Wise)
  B *2:* 397
Respect, Hindu terms of
  B *2:* 235

Responsa
  A *2:* 356
Resurrection of Jesus Christ
  B *1:* 192–93
Return concept, in Daoism
  PS 151–52
Return to Righteousness (Dharmapala)
  B *1:* 112, 120
Revelation
  A *1:* 137
Revival Shinto
  A *2:* 400
Rhea
  A *1:* 223
Rheinische Zeitung newspaper
  B *2:* 265
Rhetoric (Aristotle)
  B *1:* 39
Rhiannon
  A *2:* 380
Rig Veda
  A *2:* 251, 265
  formalization of
  A *2:* 241
Right Action
  PS 166
Right Concentration
  PS 166
Right Effort
  PS 166
Right Livelihood
  PS 166
Right Mindfulness
  PS 166
Right Speech
  PS 166
Right Thought
  PS 166
Right Understanding
  PS 166
Right View
  PS 166
Ring-stone symbol
  A *1:* 80
Rinpoche, Guru
  A *1:* 92

Rishis
  PS 113
Ritual, use of
  African indigenous religions
  A *2:* 275
  Asatru religion
  A *2:* 378
  indigenous religions
  A *2:* 273
  Shinto
  A *2:* 409–10
  Zoroastrianism
  A *2:* 456–57
Ritual impurity and cleanliness
  A *2:* 403–04
Rituals
  A *1:* 11, 79; *2:* 315–316
Roman Catholic Church
  A *1:* 132–33
Roman Catholics, number of,
  A *1:* 134
Roman emperors, cult of
  A *1:* 212
Roman Empire, in Palestine
  A *2:* 346
Romans
  festivals
  A *1:* 183
  gods and godesses of
  A *1:* 207
  See also specific gods and
  goddesses
Romulus and Remus
  A *1:* 224
Rosary beads
  A *2:* 257
Rosh Hashanah
  A *2:* 362–63
Rosicrucians
  B *1:* 139
Rowlatt Acts
  B *1:* 134
Royal Ancestral Shrine
  A *1:* 166
Ru Jia (Ju Chia)
  B *1:* 83

The Rubaiyat of Omar Kayyam
(Khayyam)
A *2:* 319
Ruben (son of Jacob)
B *1:* 6
Rudrahsha beads
A *2:* 257
"The Rule of the Orisha."
See Santería
Rushd, Ibn
B *1:* 150
Ruskin, John
B *1:* 130–31
Russell, Bertrand
A *1:* 33–34
Russia, persecution of Jews in
A *2:* 348
Russian Revolution
B *2:* 360–61
Russian Student Christian
Movement
B *2:* 361

S

Sabbah Leading the Initiations at
Alamut (Hassan)
B *1:* 146 (ill.)
Sabbat (Sabbath)
A *2:* 359
Sabbats
A *2:* 388–89
Sabr
B *1:* 13
Sacrament of Reconciliation
A *1:* 146
Sacraments
Eastern Orthodox Church
A *1:* 138–39
Roman Catholic Church
A *1:* 138–39
See also rituals
Sacred Ecology movement
PS 97
Sacred Marriage ritual
A *1:* 57

Sacred objects
A *1:* 11
Sacred Pipe
A *2:* 288
*The Sacred Pipe: Black Elk's Accont
of the Seven Rites of the Oglala
Sioux* (Black Elk)
B *1:* 52, 57
Sacred texts of Zoroastrianism
A *2:* 453
"Sacred thread"
A *2:* 257–58
Sacred writings
A *1:* 11
Sacredness, in Zoroastrianism
PS 188
Sacrifices, by Greeks and Romans
A *1:* 230–31
Sadducees
A *2:* 350
Sadhu
B *2:* 235
A *2:* 250
Saffron, symbolism of
A *2:* 255–56
"Saffronization" movement
A *2:* 269
Sage
B *2:* 235
Sahaba defined
PS 30
Sahajdharis sect
A *2:* 426
Sahib Chand
B *2:* 354
Saint Ignatius of Loyola.
See Loyola, Ignatius
Saint Mary of Paris.
See Skobtsova, Mother Maria
Saint Matthew. *See* Mathew, Saint
Saint Paul. *See* Paul, Saint
Sainthood
B *2:* 221
See also Beatification
Saivas Hinduism
A *2:* 245

Sakat (charily)
A *2:* 306
Sake, ritual use of
A *2:* 410
Saktis Hinduism
A *2:* 241, 245
Sakyamuni Buddha.
See The Buddha
Saladin
A *2:* 299, 300
Salat (daily prayer)
A *2:* 306, 310–13
Salat ul' Jumu'ah
A *2:* 313
Salba (god)
A *2:* 289
Salem Witch Trials
PS 98 (ill.)
Salt, symbolism of
A *2:* 408
Salvation
as component of religion
A *1:* 2
concept of
A *1:* 11
three ways to achieve
A *2:* 250
Sama Veda
A *2:* 251
Samhain (Samhuinn) festival
A *2:* 381, 389, 390
Samhitas (hymns)
A *2:* 251
Samsara (cycle of life)
A *2:* 247, 419
explained
PS 166
in Sikhism
PS 88
Samson and Delilah (movie)
A *2:* 368
Samurai class, influence of
Confucianism on
A *1:* 173
San Guan (San-kuan)
A *1:* 189

San Qing (San-ching)
A 1: 188
Sanatana Dharma
A 2: 239
Sanchi stupa monument
A 1: 110
Sanchita Karma
A 2: 263
Sangha, belief in
A 1: 99
Sangha Day (Magha Puja Day)
A 1: 108
Sanhedron
A 1: 122
Sankara
B 2: 237, 329
Sannyasi practice
B 2: 241–42
Sannyasins
A 2: 250
Sanskrit language
PS 88
Santería
A 2: 284 (ill.)
beliefs of
A 2: 283
creator-god in
A 2: 283
eleven commandments of
Olódùmarè
A 2: 284
names of
A 2: 282
names of clergy in
A 2: 285
rituals of
A 2: 285
See also Neo-Paganism
Santeros. See Santería
Santiago de Compostela,
pilgrimages to
A 1: 141
Sanyasa stage
A 2: 248
Saoshyant
A 2: 452

Saqqara, step pyramid at
A 1: 52
Saraasavi-Sandaresa (newspaper)
B 1: 110
Sarai (wife of Abraham)
B 1: 3–4
Sarasvati (goddess)
A 2: 259, 262
Sargon I
B 1: 123
Sargon the Great
A 1: 40
Sari
A 2: 261
Sarnath, pilgrimages to
A 1: 108
Sasaki, Sadako
A 2: 416
Sassanid Dynasty
A 2: 448
B 2: 205
Satan worship
PS 97
Satanists
A 2: 372–73
Sathyartha Prakasha (Light of Truth)
B 1: 103–04
Satori
A 1: 96
Saturnalia
A 1: 15
Saturnalia festival
A 1: 233
Satya vow
A 2: 323
PS 137
Satyagraha principles
A 2: 266
Satyar vow
B 2: 246
Saul of Tarsus, conversion of
A 1: 123
Saum (fasting)
A 2: 306
Savior figure, in Zoroastrianism
A 2: 452

Schechem plain
B 1: 3
Scheherazade, Queen
A 2: 320
Scholars, exile of
A 1: 128–29
Scholastic Confucianism
A 1: 160
School of Athens (Raphael)
B 2: 315 (ill.)
School of the Elders.
See Theravada Buddhism
School of the Scholars
B 1: 83
Schopenhauer, Arthur
A 1: 92–93
Schwärmer group
B 2: 277, 278
Science
Greek and Roman influence on
A 1: 237
Muslim contributions to
A 2: 317
rejection of
A 1: 35
universal rules observed by
A 1: 25–26
See also Enlightenment
Science, as source of reason
PS 196
Scientific method
A 1: 208, 210
Scientologists, number of
A 1: 2
Scottish Church College
B 2: 384
Scythian Shards (Mother Maria)
B 2: 360
Second Vatican Council
A 1: 130
Sects
A 1: 10
Secular Games
A 1: 233
Secularism, rise in
A 1: 130

Secularization. *See* Agnosticism;
  Atheism
Seder
  A *2:* 362
Sedreh-pushi Ceremony
  A *2:* 460, 461 (ill.)
Segal, Joshua
  B *1:* 176
Seljuks
  A *2:* 299
*A Sender of Words: Essays in
  Memory of John G. Neihardt*
  B *1:* 57
Sephardic Jews
  A *2:* 350
September 11, 2001, attacks
  A *2:* 300, 320–21, 440–41
Sermon on the Mount
  PS 122, 204, 209 (ill.)
Set (god)
  A *1:* 43, 48
Seti Pir shrine
  A *2:* 459
"Setting in Motion the Wheel of
  the Doctrine." *See* The Four
  Noble Truths of Buddhism
"Setting in Motion the Wheel of
  the Law or Truth" lesson
  A *1:* 96–97
The Seven Tables of Creation (King)
  A *1:* 49
"The Seven Voyages of Sinbad
  the Sailor"
  A *2:* 320
Seven Years in Tibet (Harrer)
  B *1:* 94
Sextus Empiricus
  A *1:* 219
Shabbat, about
  PS 6
Shabe-Yalda
  A *1:* 15
Shacharit service
  A *2:* 359
Shafi legal tradition
  PS 30

Shahadah (declaration of faith)
  A *2:* 305–06, 318 (ill.)
Shahanshahi calendar
  A *2:* 457
Shakyamuni. *See* The Buddha
Shamanism
  B *2:* 343, 344 (ill.), 349
Shamanism, in African
  indigenous religion
  A *2:* 277–78
Shamans
  A *2:* 279 (ill.)
  PS 97
  Apache
  A *2:* 289
  in art at Trois Frères,
    France
  A *1:* 5
  rise of
  A *1:* 6
  Tibetan
  A *2:* 290
Shamash (god)
  A *1:* 46
Shambala Sun newspaper
  B *2:* 360
Shangdi (god)
  A *1:* 22, 166–67
Shangs (orisha), renaming of
  A *2:* 283
Shapur I
  A *2:* 453
Shari'ah
  A *2:* 300
Shaytan/Satan
  A *2:* 305
Shehu Usman Dan Fodio.
  See Usuman Dan Fodio
Shema prayer
  A *2:* 359
Shemoneh Esrei prayer
  A *2:* 359
Shemot
  PS 11
Shenxane, Leah Nomalizo
  B *2:* 369

Shepa (god)
  A *2:* 289
Shi'a
  B *1:* 25
  See also Bahá'i
Shi'at Ali. *See* Shi'a
Shield of David. *See* Magen David
Shi'ite Muslims
  A *2:* 298, 301, 303
Shi'ite/Sunni
  conflict between
  A *2:* 298, 299
  differences between
  A *2:* 301–02
Shinbutsu bunri
  A *2:* 396
Shinjing (Shih-chine)
  A *1:* 164
Shinto
  A *2:* **393–417,** 403 (ill.)
  about
  A *2:* 399
  creation account of
  PS 3
  decline of
  A *2:* 398–99
  festivals
  A *2:* 411–12
  influence of
  A *2:* 413, 415–16
  male and female
    elements of
  PS 14
  origin of
  PS 16
  overview
  A *2:* 393–94
  ritual nature of
  A *2:* 407–08
  symbols of
  A *2:* 406–08
  See also Black Elk Speaks
Shinto Buddhism
  A *2:* 396
Shinto kami
  PS 15

Shinto shrines
   A *2:* 398, 407
Shiva (goddess)
   A *2:* 262
   B *1:* 105 (ill.)
Shiva Hinduism
   A *2:* 247
Shivaism
   A *2:* 241
Shiva's Tears
   A *2:* 257
Shivhei ha-Besht (In Praise of the
   Baal Shem Tov)
   B *1:* 177
The Shoemaker's Family (Wise)
   B *2:* 397
Shoghi Effendi (Guardian of the
   Bahá'í Faith)
   A *1:* 74–75, 76
   PS 177–78, 182
Short Obligatory Prayer
   A *1:* 83
Shravana Belgola
   A *2:* 339
Shri Dasam Granth Sahib
   (Gobind Singh)
   B *2:* 355
Shri defined
   B *2:* 235
Shrine of Bab
   A *1:* 81 (ill.), 82
   PS 182 (ill.)
Shrine of Bahá'u'lláh
   A *1:* 82
   PS 177 (ill.)
Shrine Shinto
   A *2:* 400
Shrines, made of reeds
   A *1:* 43
Shu (god)
   A *1:* 43
Shujing (Shu-ching)
   A *1:* 164
Shukr
   B *1:* 13
Shuliang He (Shu-liang Ho)
   B *1:* 85

Shwedagon stupa (Rangoon,
   Burmam/Myanmar)
   A *1:* 106
Sibbah beads
   A *2:* 257
Sick and Suffering Co-Workers
   B *2:* 294
Siddartha Guatama
   about
   A *1:* 87
   enlightenment of
   A *1:* 89
   four significant events in life
   of
   A *1:* 88
   view of in Buddhism
   A *1:* 4
   views on salvation
   A *1:* 23
   See also "Middle way";
      The Buddha
Siddha concept
   A *2:* 332
Siddhi defined
   B *2:* 253
Sigilovdda Sutra
   A *1:* 112
Sikhism
   A *2:* **419–41,** 424 (ill.)
   about
   PS 85
   beliefs of
   A *2:* 419–20
   B *2:* 352
   calendar of
   A *2:* 434–35
   ceremonies of
   A *2:* 435
   commandments of
   A *2:* 438
   conflicts within
   A *2:* 426–27
   defensive militarism
   B *2:* 351
   festivals of
   A *2:* 435–36

five K's
   B *2:* 354–55
   influence of
   A *2:* 440–41
   Jewish kosher laws and
   A *2:* 369
   origin
   B *2:* 350–51
   other religions and
   A *2:* 428–29
   rites of passage in
   A *2:* 438
   sects of
   A *2:* 425–26
   similarity to Hinduism
   PS 88
   ten gurus of
   PS 86
   See also Sri Guru Granth
      Sahib
Sikhs
   day to day life of
   A *2:* 429
   number of
   A *2:* 420
   pronunciation of
   A *2:* 419
   separatists
   A *2:* 425
Simeon (son of Jacob)
   B *1:* 6
Simon (apostle). *See* Peter
Sin (god)
   A *1:* 40, 61
"Sin" in Jainism
   PS 140–41
Sina, Ibn
   B *1:* 147
Sinfulness in daily activities
   PS 24
Singh, taking name of
   B *2:* 354
Sinhala Bauddhaya weekly
   B *1:* 112
Sins, types of
   A *1:* 146

Sioux
  foundational myth of
  PS 3
  symbols of
  PS 35–36
  See also Black Elk Speaks;
    Dakota tribe
Sioux holy men
  A *2:* 288
Sira
  B *2:* 299, 300
Sirat nabawiyya
  B *2:* 299
Sirhind executions
  B *2:* 356
Sister Mary Teresa.
  See Teresa, Mother
Sisters of Loreto
  B *2:* 292
Sistine Chapel
  A *1:* 147
Sitting Bull
  B *1:* 53
Six Arts
  B *1:* 85
  PS 130
Six Grandfathers, creation/
  foundation myths of
  PS 3
Siyyid ʿAli-Muhammad
  PS 176
Skadi (goddess)
  A *2:* 378
Skeptics school of thought
  A *1:* 219, 237
Skobtsova, Mother Maria
  B *2:* **335–42**
  canonization of
  B *2:* 341
  charitable work
  B *2:* 338
  early life
  B *2:* 335–36
  poetry of
  B *2:* 341
  travels of

B *2:* 337–38
Skullcap, wearing
  A *2:* 359, 359 (ill.)
Sky. *See specific creation stories*
Slavery, American Jewish views of
  B *2:* 396
Slavery, impact on indigenous
  religions
  A *2:* 279–80
Small Vehicle Buddhism.
  See Theravada Buddhism
Small Vows of Mahavira
  PS 145
Smartism
  A *2:* 245
Smenkhare (son of Akhenaten)
  B *1:* 14
Smerdis
  A *2:* 450
Smith, Huston
  A *1:* 96
Smyth, John
  A *1:* 134
Sobonfu, Elisabeth
  B *2:* 373
Social justice
  B *2:* 303
  PS 194
Socialism
  B *2:* 265
Society, five primary
  relationships of
  A *1:* 154
Society of Jesus (Jesuit order)
  B *2:* 220–21, 369
Socrates
  B *2:* 314, 315
  emphasis on ethics
  A *1:* 216
  execution of
  A *1:* 24
  theories of
  A *1:* 208
  trial and death of
  A *1:* 219–20
  views on knowledge

and behavior
  A *1:* 227
  See also Anaxagoras
Socratic method
  A *1:* 216
  B *2:* 329
Sodom, destruction of
  B *1:* 6
Sokagakkai
  B *2:* 311 (ill.)
Sokkuram Grotto
  A *1:* 114
Sokoto caliphate
  B *1:* 106–07, 381
Solomon (king)
  A *2:* 346
Somé, Malidoma Patrice
  B *2:* **343–50**
  early life
  B *2:* 344–45
  education
  B *2:* 345, 347–48
  profession
  B *2:* 349
Something Beautiful for God (film)
  B *2:* 294
Song Dynasty
  A *1:* 157, 185
Song Shan mountain
  A *1:* 198
Sophist (Plato)
  B *2:* 317, 331
Sophists
  A *1:* 215
Sophocles
  A *1:* 211
Sorbonne University
  B *2:* 372
"The sorcerer"
  A *1:* 5
The Sorrowful Mysteries
  A *2:* 257
Soul
  as the divine mind
  A *1:* 219
  immortality of

A *1:* 216
  primary belief in Sikhism
A *2:* 428
  three parts of
A *2:* 282
Souls, different kinds of
A *1:* 47
Souls of the dead, Roman beliefs
  about
A *1:* 235
South Africa, boycotts against,
  379
South African Council of
  Churches
B *2:* 370
South America, spread of Islam in
A *2:* 300
Southern Baptist Convention
A *1:* 134
Southern Buddhism.
  See Theravada Buddhism
"Southern School"
A *2:* 244
Southern School of Buddhism
PS 172
Soviet Union (former),
  non-believers in
A *1:* 31
Soweto (South Africa)
B *2:* 370
Spain, Judaism in
A *2:* 348
Spain, under Muslim rule
B *2:* 250
Spanish Reconquista
A *2:* 296
Sparta
B *2:* 313
Spells for Going Forth by Day
A *1:* 48
Spena Nask
B *2:* 401
Spenta Ameraiti
A *2:* 451
Spenta Ameraiti concept
PS 186

Spenta Mainyu
A *2:* 443, 451
Spenta Mainyu Gatha
PS 186
Spenta Mainyu spirit
B *2:* 402
Spentamainyush Gatha
PS 190–91
Spirit possession
A *2:* 281, 284
Spirits, in African indigenous
  religions
A *2:* 276–77
Spiritual Exercises (Loyola)
B *2:* 219, 220
Spring and Autumn Annals
  (Confucius)
A *1:* 164
B *1:* 89
PS 136
Spring Festivals
A *2:* 411
Sri Arjan Dev Ji
PS 86
Sri Guru Granth Sahib
PS 85–96, 91 (ill.)
Sri Harmandir Sahib
A *2:* 437
Sri Lanka, religious tradition in
A *1:* 94
Sri Lanka Buddhism
B *1:* 111
Sri Ramanujacharya. *See* Ramanuja
Sri Sampradaya
A *2:* 244
St. Mary's Cathedral (Johannesburg)
B *2:* 369
St. Mary's High School (Calcutta)
B *2:* 292
Stability, nature of
A *1:* 227
Stanford University
B *2:* 373
Star charting, and modern
  astronomy
A *1:* 65

Star of David. *See* Magen David
State Shinto
A *2:* 400
Statesman (Plato)
B *2:* 317, 331
Statues, gods housed in
A *1:* 43
Stoicism
A *1:* 218, 229
Stonehenge, rock timepieces at
A *1:* 15
Structure, of indigenous religions
A *2:* 273
Stupas
A *1:* 106
Subh-i Azal. *See* Mirza Yahya
Suddharma-Pundarika.
  See Mahayana Buddhism
Suddharma-Pundarika Sutra
A *1:* 100
Suddhodana
A *1:* 87
See also The Buddha
Sudras (caste)
A *2:* 263
Sufism
A *2:* 302–03
B *1:* 11, 104 (ill.), 149 (ill.);
  2: 343–44
See also Ghazālī, Abu Hamid
  Muhammad al-
Sukarnoputri, Megawati
A *2:* 320
Sukothai temples
A *1:* 106
Suleiman the Magnificent
A *2:* 364
Sultanpur (India)
PS 85
Sumer
B *1:* 121, 122
  defeat of
A *1:* 40
  organization of religion in
A *1:* 39
See also Sumerians

Sumeria, Mother Goddess in
  A *1:* 7
Sumerians
  A *1:* 39–40
Sumi-e painting style
  A *1:* 115
Sumo wrestling
  A *2:* 415 (ill.), 416
Sun, worship of
  A *1:* 230; *2:* 406
Sun goddess. *See* Amaterasu
Sun Mother
  PS 3
Sun Sumiao
  A *1:* 202
Sunday, Billy
  PS 196
Sunday school classes
  A *1:* 138
Sunga dynasty, Buddhism and
  A *1:* 92
Sunnah
  PS 30
Sunni
  B *1:* 25
Sunni Muslims
  A *2:* 298, 303
Sunni/Shi'ite
  conflict between
  A *2:* 298, 299
  differences between
  A *2:* 301–02
Sunrise Dance (Apache tribe)
  A *2:* 288 (ill.)
Sunyata principle
  A *1:* 98
Supernatural world, in African
  indigenous religions
  A *2:* 275
"Supernaturals," in Apache
  belief system
  A *2:* 289
Supplication
  A *1:* 5; *2:* 311
Supreme being
  PS 3

Supreme Unity sect
  A *1:* 185
Suras, of the Koran
  A *2:* 307
Suriname, spread of Islam in
  A *2:* 300
Sus-ano-o
  PS 21
Susano-o, sword of
  A *2:* 407
Sushruta
  A *2:* 265
Sutra, defined
  PS 137
Suttapitaka
  PS 168
Suzuki, D. T.
  A *1:* 93–94
Svetambara Jains, religious
  ceremonies of
  A *2:* 337–38
Svetambara sect
  A *2:* 328, 329
  B *2:* 249
Swami Birajananda
  B *1:* 102–03
Swami defined
  B *2:* 235
  PS 112
Swami Prabhupada
  B *2:* 244–45
Swami Vivekananda
  A *2:* 242, 266
  about
  PS 110–12
  significance of
  PS 112
Swastika symbol (Hinduism)
  A *2:* 254–55, 255 (ill.), 287
Swastika symbol (Jainism)
  A *2:* 334–35
Sweden, non-believers in
  A *1:* 31
Sweet Potato Buddhist
  community
  B *2:* 362–63

Symposium (Plato)
  A *1:* 229
Symbols
  Asatru (god)
  A *2:* 378
  Bahá'í
  A *1:* 80
  Buddhist
  A *1:* 101–02
  Christian
  A *1:* 137–38, 137 (ill.)
  Confucian
  A *1:* 164–65
  Cupid (god)
  A *1:* 230
  Daoist
  A *1:* 191–93
  Dharma wheel
  A *1:* 101 (ill.)
  Egyptian and
    Mesopotamian
  A *1:* 42, 51
  Eros (god)
  A *1:* 230
  Jain
  A *2:* 334–35
  Japanese
  A *2:* 406–08
  Judaism
  A *2:* 356–59
  Oglala Sioux
  A *2:* 287
  in religions
  A *2:* 287
  Shinto
  A *2:* 406–08
  See also specific symbols
Symposium (Plato)
  B *2:* 316
Synthetic religions
  A *2:* 271
Syria
  B *1:* 3
The System of Nature
  (d'Holbach)
  A *1:* 26, 32

T

Tadhkirat al-Awliya (Biographies of the Saints)
  B *1:* 10
Taga shrine
  A *2:* 406
Tagore, Rabindranath
  B *1:* 133
Tahafut al-Tahafut
  (Ibn Rushd)
  B *1:* 150
Tai Shan mountain
  A *1:* 198
Tai shen spirit
  A *1:* 200
Taijichuan (tai chi)
  A *1:* 199–200
Taijiquan (tai chi)
  A *1:* 187
Taino Indians
  A *2:* 280
Taiping Dao
  A *1:* 184
Taiping Jing (Tai-p'ing Ching)
  A *1:* 191
Taiping Rebellion
  A *1:* 184
Takht Damdama
  A *2:* 437
Takht Hazoor
  A *2:* 438
Takht Keshgarh
  A *2:* 437
Takht Patna
  A *2:* 438
Tales from the Kohiki
  PS 13–22
Talismans
  B *2:* 372 (ill.), 373
Tallit, wearing
  A *2:* 359, 359 (ill.)
Talmud
  A *2:* 356
  B *2:* 392

See also specific parts of the Talmud
Talwandi Sabor
  B *2:* 356
Tamil Sangam
  A *2:* 265
Tammuz (god)
  A *1:* 49
Tanakh (Hebrew Bible)
  PS 5–12
  Christian Bible and
  PS 203
  creation account in
  PS 2
  dating of
  PS 11
  parts of
  PS 5
  style of
  PS 6
Tanakh (Torah)
  A *2:* 354–55
  B *2:* 283, 392
  Christianity and
  A *1:* 123–24
  Judaism and
  A *2:* 346
Tang Dynasty
  A *1:* 157, 181
Tanis
  A *1:* 45
Tantras
  A *1:* 95
Tantric branch of
  Buddhism
  A *1:* 95
Tantrism
  B *1:* 140
Tao chiao. *See* Religious Daoism
The Tao of Physics: An Exploration of the Parallels Between Modern Physics and Eastern Mysticiam (Capra)
  A *1:* 206
Tao Te Ching. *See* Dao De Jing
Taoism. *See* Daoism

Taranis
  A *2:* 380
Tartaros
  A *1:* 223
Tawba
  B *1:* 13
Tawhid
  B *1:* 13
Taxes, in Muslim lands
  A *2:* 296–97
Teachers' Day
  PS 135
Tefilah prayer
  A *2:* 359–60
Tefnut (god)
  A *1:* 43
Teg Bahadur (Guru)
  A *2:* 423, 427
  B *1:* 155
  PS 86
Tel el-Amarna
  B *1:* 11
Tell el-Amarna
  A *1:* 46
Temnu (emperor)
  A *2:* 395, 404–05
Temple
  desecration of
  A *2:* 346
  destruction of
  A *2:* 346, 348
Temple complexes
  in Mesopotamia
  A *1:* 40
  in Ranakpur, India
  A *2:* 328
Temple worship
  A *2:* 337 (ill.)
Temples of Confucianism
  A *1:* 166
Ten Commandments
  A *2:* 346
  PS 206
Ten Commandments (movie)
  A *2:* 368
Ten Commandments tablet
  B *2:* 288–89, 288 (ill.)

Tendai Buddhism
  B *2:* 312
Tenrikyo Shinto
  A *2:* 401
Tenri-o-No-Mikoto, creator-god
  concept and
  A *2:* 401
Tenzin Gyatso
  A *1:* 92
  See also Dalai Lama
Terah (father of Abraham)
  B *1:* 2
Teresa, Mother
  B *2:* **351–58,** 351 (ill.)
  beatified
  B *2:* 356–57
  charity work
  B *2:* 353–54
  early life
  B *2:* 352
  honors for
  B *2:* 354–55
Teresa of Avila
  B *2:* 292
Tesla, Nikola
  B *2:* 384
Tetzel, Johann
  B *2:* 225
Thailand
  religious tradition in
  A *1:* 94
  spread of Buddhism in
  A *1:* 92
Thales
  A *1:* 213, 226
  B *1:* 26
  modern astronomy and
  A *1:* 237
Thathana Yeiktha meditation
  center
  B *1:* 117–18
Theocracy, in Mesopotamia and
  Egypt
  A *1:* 37
Theocracy defined
  B *1:* 79

Theodosius I
  A *1:* 125
Theogony (Hesiod)
  A *1:* 210, 228
Theological Academy of the
  Alexander Nevsky Monastery
  B *2:* 360
Theological Education Fund
  B *2:* 369
Theosophical Society
  B *1:* 109, 139
Theravada Buddhism
  A *1:* 90, 93–94
  B *1:* 73–74; *2:* 311–12
  PS 167–68, 172
Thich Nhat Hanh
  B *2:* **359–65,** 359 (ill.)
  early life
  B *2:* 360
  exile
  B *2:* 361–62
"Third Moses." *See* Mendelssohn,
  Moses
Thirteen Classics (Confucius)
  A *1:* 164
Thirty Tyrants
  B *2:* 313–14, 327–28
Thirty Years' War
  B *2:* 231
Thodosius I, polytheism banned by
  A *1:* 212
Thomas Aquinas (Saint)
  B *1:* 150
Thor (god)
  A *2:* 377
Thoreau, Henry David
  A *1:* 93
  B *1:* 130
Thoth (god)
  A *1:* 42
Thought, unified system of
  A *1:* 1
A Thousand and One Nights
  A *2:* 319
  B *1:* 12
Three dots symbol

  A *2:* 334
Three jewels code
  B *2:* 253
Three Jewels of Buddhism
  A *1:* 99
Three Jewels of Daoism
  A *1:* 187
Three Jewels of Jainism
  A *2:* 333, 334
Three Officials
  A *1:* 189
Three Primordials (Principals)
  A *1:* 189
Three Pure Ones
  A *1:* 188, 197
Three Refuges recitation
  B *1:* 72
Three Wise Men (Magi)
  A *2:* 447
"Threefold path," of Zoroastrians
  A *2:* 452
  PS 186
Thus Spake Zarathustra
  (Nietzsche)
  A *1:* 28
Tian/Heaven
  A *1:* 22
Tianming (t'ien-ming)
  B *1:* 85–86
Tianshi Dao. *See* Daoism
Tibet
  Buddhism in
  A *1:* 92
  Chinese invasion of
  B *1:* 94–95
  religious tradition in
  A *1:* 95
  See also Bon religion; Dalai
  Lama
Tibetan Book of the Dead
  A *1:* 100
Tibetan Buddhism
  B *1:* 92, 94
  physical reincarnation belief
  A *1:* 99
  in Tibet

A *1:* 92
in the United States
A *1:* 94
Tibetan Institute of Performing
Arts
B *1:* 96
Tigris River
A *1:* 39
Tilaka
A *2:* 261
Tillich, Paul
A *1:* 1, 28–29
Timaeus (Plato)
A *1:* 229
B *2:* 317, 331
Time
cyclical nature of in Daoism
A *1:* 185
cyclical nature of in Jainism
A *2:* 325
Jain concept of
A *2:* 325
Time International
B *2:* 364
Timur
B *1:* 168
Tipitaka text
PS 168, 172 (ill.)
Tipitakas
A *1:* 99–100
Tirthankara
B *2:* 244–45
Tirthankara, defined
PS 139–40
Tirthankara figures
A *2:* 325–26, 329–30
Tirthankaras
PS 139 (ill.)
Tithing, in Sikhism
A *2:* 437
Tiy (mother of Akhenaten)
B *1:* 10, 13
Toharot (Purities)
A *2:* 356
Tolerance of other faiths, in
Bahá'í faith

A *1:* 78
Tolstoy, Leo
B *1:* 130
Tolstoy Farm
B *1:* 133
Tonpa Shenrab Miwo
A *2:* 289
Torah
B *2:* 212 (ill.), 278
PS 5
See also Leibowitz, Nechama;
Tanakh
Torah (Law)
A *2:* 354–55
See also Tanakh
Tori symbol
A *2:* 407, 408 (ill.)
Totems
A *1:* 6
Towers of Silence
A *2:* 461
Townships
B *2:* 380 (ill.)
Trade, and rise of Islam
A *2:* 296
Traditional Healer
A *2:* 278
Traditions, reintroduction of
A *1:* 155
Transmigration of the soul
A *2:* 247
Trayi Veda
A *2:* 251
Treatise on Alchemy
(Sun Sumiao)
A *1:* 202
"Treatise on the Good"
A *2:* 265
Treindriya beings
A *2:* 331
Trials, in the afterlife
A *1:* 48
Trinity
doctrine of
A *1:* 126, 136
Neoplatonism and

A *1:* 236
Trois Frères (France)
A *1:* 5
"True Classic of Perfect
Emptiness"
A *1:* 191
Truth and Reconciliation
Commission (South Africa)
B *2:* 373
Tsuki-Yumi
PS 3, 21
TULIP. *See* Five Points of
Calvinism
TulKubra, Khadijah.
See Khadijah
Tung Zhong-shu
A *1:* 156–57
Tunis
B *1:* 167 (ill.), 168
Turban tying rite
A *2:* 438
Turkey
European Union and
A *2:* 320
Mother Goddess worship in
A *1:* 6
Turkish Muslims
A *2:* 299
Turning of the Wheel of Law or
Truth
A *1:* 108
Tutankhamen (son of Akhenaten)
B *1:* 13
Tutankhatan. *See* Tutankhamen
(son of Akhenaten)
Tutu, Desmond Mpilo
B *2:* **367–74,** 367 (ill.)
career in education
B *2:* 373
early life and education
B *2:* 368–69
honors awarded to
B *2:* 371
religious life
B *2:* 369–70, 373
Twelfth Imam
B *1:* 43

Twelve Limbs texts
  A *2:* 334
The Twelve Tribes of Israel (Chagall)
  A *2:* 369
Twelve vows
  A *2:* 340
"Typical" Parsi Zoroastrianism
  A *2:* 450
Tzaddick, creation of
  B *1:* 182
Tzitzit, wearing
  A *2:* 359

U

U.S. Presidential Medal of
  Freedom
  B *2:* 295
Udasis sect
  A *2:* 426
Udupi. *See* Madhva
Uijain (city)
  A *2:* 260
Umar (second caliph)
  B *1:* 29
Umar caliph
  A *2:* 298
Umayyad caliphate
  (Córdoba, Spain)
  A *2:* 296, 348
Umayyad rule
  B *1:* 30
Umayyads
  A *2:* 298
Umm Kulthum (daughter of
  Fatima)
  B *1:* 27
Unification, Qur'an as factor in
  PS 26
Unified Buddhist Church
  B *2:* 362
Union of American Hebrew
  Congregations
  B *2:* 391, 393, 394–95
Unitarian Bahá'ís
  A *1:* 76

Unitarianism Universalism,
  beliefs of
  A *1:* 19
United Nations, and Bahá'í
  influences
  A *1:* 84–85
United Nations Development
  Fund for Women
  A *1:* 85
United States, non-believers in
  A *1:* 31
Unities of Bahá'í
  PS 175–76
Unity
  importance of in Qur'an
  PS 26
  of Wiccans
  PS 100
Unity symbol
  A *2:* 287–88
Universal cosmic rule, concept of
  A *1:* 19
Universal House of Justice
  A *1:* 74
Universal Salvation
  A *1:* 196
Universe
  creation of
  A *1:* 226; *2:* 378
  PS 23
  cyclical nature of
  A *1:* 228
  five parts of
  A *2:* 332
  Jain diagram of
  PS 143 (ill.)
  nature of
  PS 3, 110, 138
  See also Creation Stories
University of Johannesburg
  B *2:* 377
University of Michigan
  B *2:* 373
"Untouchables" (caste)
  A *2:* 263
  B *2:* 236

Upanishads
  A *2:* 242, 251, 252
  B *2:* 385–86
  PS 111
Uposatha, in Theravada
  Buddhism
  A *1:* 105
Upper Pure
  A *1:* 188
Ur
  A *1:* 40
  B *1:* 2, 122, 123
Uranus (god)
  A *1:* 223
  PS 2, 3
Uruk
  B *1:* 122
Uruk, temple complex in
  A *1:* 40
Ushtavaiti Gatha
  PS 190
Usmani Qur'ans
  A *2:* 309
  PS 29
Ussher, John
  A *1:* 28
Ustavaiti Gatha
  PS 186
Uthman (caliph)
  A *2:* 298, 308
Uthman (third caliph)
  B *1:* 29
Utu (sun god)
  B *1:* 122
Utu/Shamash (sun god)
  A *1:* 37
Usuman Dan Fodio
  B *2:* **375–82**
  caliphate
  B *2:* 379–80
  death of
  B *2:* 381
  Degal (city)
  B *2:* 377
  early life
  B *2:* 376

effects of war on Degal
  B *2:* 380–81
emmigration to Gudu
  B *2:* 378
legacy
  B *2:* 381
Uzerin
  A *2:* 456

V

Vahisto Ishti Gatha
  PS 186
Vaidika Dharma
  A *2:* 239
Vaishnavaism Hinduism
  A *2:* 241, 244
Vaisyas (caste)
  A *2:* 263
Vajra (thunderbolt)
  A *1:* 102
Vajrayana/Tantra Buddhism
  A *1:* 92, 94, 95
Valesquez, Juan
  B *2:* 218
Valiente, Doreen
  B *1:* 140
Van Biema, David
  B *1:* 1
Vanaprastha stage
  A *2:* 248
Vanir class
  A *2:* 377
Varada mudra
  A *1:* 109
Vardhamana. *See* Mahavira
Vartamana Karma
  A *2:* 263
Vassa
  A *1:* 108
Vata (movement energy)
  A *2:* 268
Vatican City, pilgrimages to
  A *1:* 141
Vedanta. *See* Upanishads

Vedantic philosophy
  B *2:* 388–89
Vedas
  B *1:* 105
  PS 111, 113
Vedic Period of Hinduism
  A *2:* 241–42
Vegetarianism
  A *1:* 110, 198; *2:* 265, 327, 460
Venerable Bede
  B *2:* 307
Veneration, practice of in
  Buddhism
  A *1:* 102–03
Venus (goddess)
  A *1:* 122, 230
Venus of Willendorf
  A *1:* 7
Verse of the Throne
  A *2:* 304
Vesak. *See* Wesak holy day
Veshiti
  A *2:* 261
Vesta (goddess)
  A *1:* 122, 231
Vestal Virgins
  A *1:* 231
Via Dolorosa, pilgrimages to
  A *1:* 141
Vietnam, civil wars in
  B *2:* 360
Vietnam, religious tradition in
  A *1:* 95
Vietnam Confucianism
  A *1:* 173–74
Vigil service, Orthodox Church
  A *1:* 145
Violence, controlling
  PS 187
Vipassana meditation
  B *1:* 119
Virgil
  A *1:* 211
Vishnu (Krishna) god
  A *2:* 247, 262
  B *2:* 239

PS 119
worship of
  A *2:* 244
Vishtaspa (king of Bactria)
  A *2:* 447, 453
  B *2:* 403
Visvambhar Mishra. *See* Caitanya
  Mahaprabhu
Vivekananda Illam
  B *2:* 388 (ill.)
Vivekananda Rock Memorial
  B *2:* 387
Vivekananda, Swami
  B *2:* **383–90,** 383 (ill.)
early life
  B *2:* 384–85
"Paper on Hinduism" speech
  B *2:* 387–88
religious education
  B *2:* 385–86
travels
  B *2:* 386–87, 388–89
Vivekananda Vedanta Society
  B *2:* 389
  PS 118
Vodou
  A *2:* 280–82
African influence on
  A *2:* 280–81
number of practitioners
  A *2:* 280
religious traditions in
  A *2:* 280
rituals of
  A *2:* 281
roots of
  A *2:* 279
stereotypes about
  A *2:* 282
  See also Neo-Paganism
Vohu Khshathra Gatha
  PS 186
Vohu Manah
  A *2:* 451, 452
Vohu Manah concept
  PS 186

Vologeses I
  A *2:* 453
Voltaire
  B *2:* 275
Von Westphalan, Jenny.
  See Marx, Karl
Voodoo. *See* Vodou
Vor Sior
  A *2:* 376
Vulcan
  A *1:* 122
Vyasa Krishna Dwaipayana
  A *2:* 251

W

Wailing Wall
  A *2:* 364–65
Wakan Tanka
  B *1:* 56
Wakan tanka energy
  A *2:* 288
Wakan-Tanka force
  A *2:* 410
Wang Bi (Wang Pi)
  A *1:* 184
Wang Wei
  A *1:* 174
Wang Xianzhi
  A *1:* 204
Wang Xizhi
  A *1:* 204
War Bonnet, Katie
  B *1:* 55
Warring States Period
  A *1:* 155
  PS 130
"Water person" in Dagara culture
  B *2:* 370
"Water-bodied" beings
  A *2:* 330
Watts, Alan
  A *1:* 94
"Way of devotion"
  A *2:* 250

"Way of knowledge"
  A *2:* 250
Way of Saint James,
  pilgrimages to
  A *1:* 141
Way of the Celestial Masters
  movement
  A *1:* 179
Way of the Five Pecks of Rice
  A *1:* 179
Way of the Great Peace
  A *1:* 184
"The Way of the Yellow Emperor
  and the Old Master"
  A *1:* 179
"Way of work"
  A *2:* 250
Wazir Khan
  B *1:* 160
Wedding rites
  A *2:* 439, 460
Weddings
  Christian
  A *1:* 143–44
  Daoist
  A *1:* 200
  Jewish
  A *2:* 365–66
  Shinto
  A *2:* 412
Weiss, Issac Mayer. *See* Wise,
  Isaac Mayer
Wen principle
  A *1:* 162
Wenshu
  A *1:* 95, 103
Wesak Festival
  B *1:* 109 (ill.), 112
Wesak holy day
  A *1:* 107–08
Wesley, John
  A *1:* 134
Western Wall
  A *2:* 364–65
"What is Hinduism"?
  (Vivekananda)

  A *2:* 242
What Is Religion?
  A *1:* 1–17
Wheel-turning mudra
  A *1:* 109
Whirling Dervishes
  A *2:* 303
  See also Sufism
White Cloud Daoist Monastery,
  pilgrimages to
  A *1:* 198
White Cloud Monastery
  A *1:* 185
Why I Am Not a Christian
  (Russell)
  A *1:* 33
Wicasa wakan
  A *2:* 288
Wicca
  B *1:* 142–43
  beliefs of
  A *2:* 385–86
  calendar of
  A *2:* 388–89
  legal status of
  A *2:* 390–91
  magic in
  A *2:* 385
  origins of
  A *2:* 384–85
  tools of
  A *2:* 387–88
*Wicca: A Guide for the Solitary
  Practitioner*
  PS 97–107
  about
  PS 97–98
  characteristics of
  PS 98–99
  core values of
  PS 100–01
  masculine and feminine
    principles in
  PS 3
  numbers of
  PS 106

practice rites of
PS 100
teachings of
PS 99
Wiccans
A *2:* 373
Wiezmann, Chaim
A *2:* 367–68
Wilberforce, Samuel
A *1:* 29
Wilkinson, Gardner
B *1:* 16
Winged bull
A *1:* 51
Winter solstice celebrations
A *1:* 15, 166
Wise, Isaac Mayer
B *2:* 391–97,
391 (ill.)
early life
B *2:* 392
political views
B *2:* 396
reforms by
B *2:* 392–93
temples led by
B *2:* 393
writings of
B *2:* 396–97
Wise Men. *See* Magi biblical
story
Wish-granting mudra
A *1:* 109
Witchcraft. *See* Wicca
Witchcraft Today (Gardner)
B *1:* 141
*Witchcraft: The Witch Cult in
Western Europe* (Murray)
B *1:* 141
Women, equality of in
Zoroastrianism
PS 188
Women, views of in Jainism
A *2:* 328–29
Women in early Arabian society
B *1:* 194–95

Wooley, Sir Leonard
B *1:* 124
"Words of the Doctrine."
See The Dhammapada
Works and Days (Hesiod)
A *1:* 210–11, 228
The Works of Shams of Tabriz
(Rūmī)
B *1:* 182
Workweek
A *1:* 63, 146
World
creation of
A *1:* 28
phases of in
Zoroastrianism
A *2:* 452
six categories of
PS 138
three phases of
PS 188–89
World Buddhist Congress
A *1:* 102
World Council of Churches
B *2:* 369
World Parliament of Religions
PS 109, 112, 119
World Parliament of Religions
(1893)
A *1:* 93–94; *2:* 242, 266,
328
B *1:* 111; *2:* 386, 387–88
World Peace City. *See* Lumbini,
Nepal
World Soul
A *1:* 219
World War I, opposition to
PS 195
World War II
genocide of Jews during
A *2:* 349
Sikh soldiers in
A *2:* 424
Worldly possessions, views of
A *2:* 329
Worship, forms of

A *1:* 138–39, 230–31
Wounded Knee battle
B *1:* 55
Wovoka (Paiute tribe)
B *1:* 55
Writings
PS 5
Wu wei, concept of
A *1:* 187
Wu wei, emphasis on in Daoism
PS 150

X

Xenophanes
A *1:* 23, 214
Xerxes
B *2:* 313
Xiaojing (Hsiao-ching)
A *1:* 164
Xuan xue (hsuan hsueh).
See "Dark learning"
Xun Zi
A *1:* 159, 160

Y

Yadava Prakash
B *2:* 328
Yadz region of Iran, pilgrimages to
A *2:* 459
Yahya, Mirza
B *1:* 44
Yajur Veda
A *2:* 251
Yamaga Soko
A *1:* 173
Yamuna River
A *2:* 260
Yamunacharya
B *2:* 329–30
Yan Zhen-sai (Yen Chen-sai)
B *1:* 85
Yang Zhu
A *1:* 156

Yaoyorozu no Kami
  A *2:* 402
Yarmulke, wearing
  A *2:* 359, 359 (ill.)
Yasna
  A *2:* 453
  B *2:* 400–01
  PS 185, 190
Yathrib (Medina)
  B *1:* 27; *2:* 303, 305
Year, division of
  A *1:* 197
Yellow Emperor's Classic on
  Medicine
  A *1:* 203
Yijing (Classic of Changes)
  A *1:* 164, 191
Yin-Yang symbol
  A *1:* 165, 191, 193
Yoga
  A *1:* 95; *2:* 248–49, 266–67,
  267 (ill.)
  PS 119
Yom Kippur
  A *2:* 363
Yoshizawa, Akira
  A *2:* 416
Yuanshi Tianzong
  (First Principle)
  A *1:* 188
Yuhuang (Jade Emperor)
  A *1:* 188
Yule
  A *2:* 388
Yunfa
  B *2:* 378
Yun-kang caves (China),
  pilgrimages to
  A *1:* 110

Z

Zarah, Abu Halah Hind, Ibn
  B *1:* 194
Zarathrutra. *See* Zarathushtra

Zarathushtra
  A *2:* 443, 447 (ill.)
  B *2:* **399–406,** 399 (ill.)
  PS 186 (ill.), 191
  in Bactria
  B *2:* 403–05
  dating of
  B *2:* 400
  early life
  B *2:* 401–02
  life of
  A *2:* 445–47
  marriage and family life
  B *2:* 404
  names of
  B *2:* 399
  religious beliefs
  B *2:* 402
  travels
  B *2:* 402–03
Zartosht. *See* Zarathushtra
Zartosht No-Diso
  A *2:* 459
Zartoshti
  A *2:* 443
Zaynab (daughter of Fatima)
  B *1:* 27
Zealots
  A *2:* 346, 350–51
Zebulun (son of Jacob)
  B *1:* 6
Zen Buddhism
  A *1:* 92, 93–94, 95–96,
  99, 115
  B *2:* 312
Zen Doctrine of Emptiness/Void
  A *1:* 115
Zend (Zand) Avesta
  A *2:* 453
  See also Avesta
Zennichi. *See* Nichiren
Zeno of Citium
  A *1:* 218
Zera'im (Seeds)
  A *2:* 356
Zeus

  A *1:* 221, 223, 230
Zhang Daoling (Chang Tao-ling)
  A *1:* 179, 182, 186
Zhang Guolao (god)
  A *1:* 190
Zhang Zhue (Chang Chueh)
  A *1:* 184
Zhongli Quan (god)
  A *1:* 190
Zhongyong (Chung Yung)
  A *1:* 163
Zhou (Chou) Dynasty
  A *1:* 22, 154–55
  PS 135
Zhu Xi
  A *1:* 157, 171
Zhuangzi
  A *1:* 178, 189, 191
Zhung Yuan festival
  A *1:* 196
Ziggurats
  A *1:* 40, 52, 52 (ill.)
  B *1:* 122
Zionism movement
  A *2:* 348
Zipporah
  B *2:* 286
Zombies
  A *2:* 282
Zoroaster. *See* Zarathushtra
Zoroastrian priest
  B *2:* 404 (ill.)
Zoroastrianism
  A *2:* **443–63**
  B *2:* 404, 404 (ill.), 405
  about
  A *2:* 446
  beliefs of
  A *2:* 451, 452
  decline of
  A *2:* 461–62
  Judaism and
  A *2:* 462
  monotheism of
  PS 188
  moral basis for

PS 122
overview
A *2:* 443–44
sects of
A *2:* 449–50
similarity to Christianity/
  Islam/Judaism
PS 191–92
supreme being in creation stories

PS 3
symbols of
PS 191
texts of
PS 187–88
See also Avesta; Gathas; Yasna
Zoroastrians
number of
A *2:* 443–44

persecution of
A *2:* 448–49
B *2:* 405
Zuhd
B *1:* 13
Zurvanism sect
A *2:* 449
Zwingli, Huldrych
A *1:* 133